The Spirit Of Fanaticism

him, without any Hefitation, he faid unto him, Thou, Sir, are the Man; upon which the Wretch trembled, and grew Pale.

Not long after, he was Conven'd before the Privy Council, and the Duke of *Lauderdale*, his Majefty's High Commiffioner then fitting in Council, but he would confefs nothing before them; which made the Right Honourable Board depute a Committee for his farther Examination: Before which he freely confefs'd the Fact, and afterwards acknowledged and fign'd his Confeffion before the King's High Commiffioner fitting in Council, with the Lord Halton the Treafurer Deputy, the Earl of Rothes Lord Chancellor, and fome other of the Council Subfcrib'd as Witneffes; and this Paper was brought at his Tryal againft him as a *judicial* Confeffion of his Crime.

After this Examination of him before his Majefty's High Commiffioner fitting in Council (which happened in *February* 1674) he was put upon his Tryal in the Criminal Court. But after his *Indictment* was read, he deny'd it, and retracted the Confeffion, which he had freely made without any promife of Pardon before the High Commiffioner, and the Council; upon which Sir *John Nisbet*, his Majefty's *Advocate* (who, notwithftanding his fair Pretenfions to the Church, either Loves or Fears the *Fanatical Faction* too much) feem'd very much furpriz'd, and defifted immediately from his Profecution, defiring the Judges to Adjourn the Court; and from that time would never purfue the Murderous Villain again, although he was oblig'd by his Office to do it, as well as by the Archbifhop; who *in Caufa Sanguinis* would not purfue him himfelf. The Judges alfo at that time had no great Stomach to fit upon the Tryal of this bloody Saint : So that the Privy-Council were forced to fend him Prifoner to the *Baffe* (a Rock in the *Forth*) where he continued till the latter End of *December*, when the Privy-Council fent for him to be Try'd again.

About this Time it was rumour'd about Town and Country, that the *Whigs* (for fo we call *Fanaticks*) defign'd to take off both the Archbifhops, and fome other Bifhops by Affaffination; and likewife vehement Sufpicions and Prefumptions were found, that they had the like Defign on other eminent Perfons, who were moft concern'd, and refolv'd to fee them reduc'd to Order and Obedience. And therefore the Council thought it expedient, to prevent fuch barbarous Attempts, and fecure the Lives of his Majefty's faithful Minifters, to bring Mr. *Mitchel* to publick Juftice, that the

Re-

Remonstrator-Presbyterians of our Country might fee, what their Clements and Ravillacs were to expect.

Since the Duke of Lauderdale came last hither, Sir John Nisbet resign'd his Charge, and his Majesty put Sir George Mackenzy, a Learned and Worthy Gentlemen into his Place; who in Obedience to the Order of the Privy-Council, pursu'd this common Enemy of Mankind, with a Courage and Zeal, that became such a gallant Man, and a good Christian, although he forefaw, he must for ever disoblige that implacable Party, which hath sworn to extirpate Episcopacy here.

You may easily judge with what Deliberation and Caution this Miscreant's Proceſs was made; seeing his Tryal was dependant four Days: For he was Arraign'd on Monday the Seventh of January in the Morning, and receiv'd not Sentence till the following Thurfday at Two in the Afternoon. As the Privy Council were very Just, so were they exceeding Merciful to this inhuman Man: For at the inſtance of his Majesty's Advocate, they commanded Sir George Lockhart, one of the best Lawyers of this Nation, to be of his Council; and had he been the greatest Subject of the three Kingdoms, his Cause could not have been more ſtrenuouſly defended, nor his Proceſs made with more Care.

The first Day was ſpent in reading the Indictment, and diſcuſſing ſome preparatory Doubts, neceſſary to be determin'd by an Interlocutory Sentence, before the Jury could be Impannell'd, and the Witneſſes Sworn. The Doubts were three: Firſt, Whether that Confeſſion, which the Priſoner made before the King's High Commiſſioner, and the Privy-Council ſitting in Council, were Judicial or Extrajudicial? The Second was, Whether if this Confeſſion ſhould be made appear to be upon hopes or promiſe of Pardon, it ſhould not ſerve for the Priſoner's Exculpation? And the Third was, Whether by a certain Act of Parliament made for the Security of his Majesty's Privy Counſellors and Officers, the attempted Aſſaſſinage of the Primate, who was a Privy-Counſellor, were Capital, or no? All which Preliminaries, the Judges deliberated upon, and Debated among themſelves on Tueſday, and on Wednefday following pronounced their Interlocutory Sentence in the Affirmative upon the ſeveral Heads.

After the Sentence was pronounc'd, the Jury was Impannell'd, and the Witneſſes Sworn; ſome of whoſe Depoſitions I ſhall ſet down as I heard them.

The Keeper of the * Tolbooth's Son Depon'd, That having ask'd the Priſoner, how he could do ſuch a Barbarous Action

* The Prifon.

1   in

in cold Blood, againſt a Man that had never done him wrong? He Anſwer'd, That it was not done in cold Blood; for the Blood of the Saints was reaking yet at the *Croſs* in *Edinburgh*. By the *Saints* he meant the *Rebels* at *Pentland-Hills* in 1666. One of which he himſelf had been; and ſome Principals whereof, that were taken in the Field, had been Executed about two Years before at the *Croſs* in *Edinburgh*.

The Lord Biſhop of *Galloway* (whom no good Churchman here ought to mention without Honour and Reſpect) having firſt aſſerted the Privilege that is granted to Biſhops, to have their Depoſitions taken at home, according to the Civil and Canon-Law; and proteſted that his Obedience to the Court ſhould be no prejudice to that Privilege; Depon'd, That having ask'd the Priſoner, What mov'd him to make ſuch a Bloody Attempt on an Innocent Man? He Anſwer'd, That he did it, becauſe he apprehended him to be an Enemy to the People of God.

The Lord *Halton* Depoſed, That having ask'd him, how he durſt be ſo wicked, as to do ſuch an execrable Fact? He anſwer'd, That he did it, becauſe the Archbiſhop was an Enemy to the Godly People of the *Weſt*.

Furthermore, the Lord Chancellor and the Lord *Halton*, teſtify'd upon Oath, That he own'd the Confeſſion produc'd in Court before the Privy Council, and acknowledged their Names, which were Subſcrib'd under it, and the Priſoner could not deny his.

Theſe Depoſitions being taken, there was no way left to ſave the Priſoner, but by making it appear, that he had made this Confeſſion upon Promiſe, or Hopes of Pardon; and therefore his Advocates deſir'd, that the Lord Chancellor might be call'd to declare upon Oath, if he did not encourage him to confeſs upon Promiſe, or Oath, to endeavour to ſecure Life and Limb, as he alledg'd his Lordſhip did. But he declar'd upon the Oath he had taken, that he never made any ſuch Promiſe or Oath unto him: And the Duke of *Lauderdale* and the Lord *Halton* being alſo call'd to Depone upon that particular, Teſtify'd, That they never knew, that the Lord Chancellor, or any other, had encourag'd him to make that Confeſſion upon Hopes or Promiſe of Pardon; which if it could have been legally prov'd, he muſt have been Abſolv'd.

The impudent Villain likewiſe deſir'd the Judges, that the Primate himſelf might be cited into the Court, to declare upon Oath, if he did not encourage him to confeſs upon a Promiſe to endeavour to procure his Pardon; to which being Sworn, he anſwer'd, That immediately after his

Appre-

Apprehenfion, he took him afide to Difcourfe with him in Private, where he did affure him he forgave him, and would endeavour to fave him from publick Juftice, if he would confefs the Fact; but that upon this Encouragement, he would make no Confeffion, nor ever after offer'd any to him; fo that tho' he ftill forgave him, yet he did not conceive himfelf bound to endeavour his Prefervation after more than five Years Obftination in his Crime.

There were many other Witneffes ready to Depone, of which there was no need. One of them could have teftify'd. That he heard him fay, that he would do the Fact, if it were to be done again: And another could have Depon'd, that he heard him fay, Let me but Shoot at him again, and I'll be content to be Hang'd if I mifs. The *Jury*, which confifted of Fifteen Gentlemen, unanimoufly found him Guilty; and when Sentence was pronounc'd, That he fhould be carried to the common Place of Execution, and there be Hang'd, he told the Judges, that he took it as from GOD, but not from them.

Since he was Condemn'd, he defir'd that fome Conventicle Minifters that were Imprifon'd with him, might be admitted to give him Comfort, and obftinately refufed the Affiftance of the Minifters of our Church. However, one of them went to him to remind him of the Murder he was Guilty of in the Eyes of God, tho' he fuffer'd him not to effectuate his Defign. But inftead of making any impreffion on his hardned Heart, or receiving common acknowledgments for his good Will, he received nothing from him but Reproaches; being told by him that he was a Murderer of Souls, and had the Blood of Souls to anfwer for, with many more Rude and Enthufiaftick Expreffions.

He was a lean hollow-cheek'd Man, of a turbulent Countenance, and had the Air of an *Affaffin* as much as a Man could have. He came with his Perriwig Powder'd to the Bar, and behav'd himfelf there, with as much Affurance as Men devoted to do Mifchief by their Principles and Complexion, refolve beforehand always to do.

As for his Original, 'tis fo obfcure, that the mean Proletarian Condition of his Parents affords me no Notice of his Birth. And for his Education, after he had paffed through the fubfidiary part of Learning, he was fent to the *College* of *Edinburgh* in the time of the late Ufurpation; where he made very fmall progrefs in any part of good Literature, but apply'd himfelf to the reading of fuch filly *Fanatical* Books, as were fit for his narrow Capacity and Enthufiaftical Temper; fo that the acquir'd, or artificial Part of *Fanati-*
cifm

ism (which *Whigs* call Grace) being added to his Nature, he might qualifie himself for Employment and Reputation, especially among the *Remonstrator-Presbyterians*, who were then the principal Part of the *Kirk.* This Faction, especially in the West, was advanc'd so far towards Enthusiasm, that they despised and suspected Men of Learning and Sense, and began to look upon it as a stinting of the Spirit, to spend any Study or Time in preparing themselves to Preach. The People especially were so possessed with this Opinion, that if they came to know, that their Ministers Preconceiv'd, much more Penn'd their Sermons in their Studies, they thought it a sufficient ground of with-drawing from them; as believing it utterly impossible, to receive any Spiritual Benefit from such carnal Sermons, as were Compos'd by the help of Study and Books.

Among these People it was, that *Mitchel* design'd to Teach and Preach; and therefore after he was graduated Master (which is here at the End of four Years) he apply'd himself to the Study of Popular Divinity under Mr. *David Dickson*, a great Apostle of the Solemn League and Covenant; under whom he continued his Method of Reading Modern *Fanatical* Pamphlets, that he might be an able Workman, and compleatly finish'd with all those *Canting* Affected Phrases, which discriminate a Spiritual from a Carnal Preacher among our *Presbyterians :* And are Musick and Charms to their Enthusiastical Ears. And that he might add the Practical to the Speculative part of *Fanaticism*, and be perfectly Master of his Trade, he frequented those private Meetings, where Conferences, Prayers and Sermons were spoken in that Dialect; and where Tone, Grimace, and Gesticulations, are far more Powerful than all the true Learning and Eloquence in the World.

Having acted sometime in these Nurseries of Enthusiasm, he thought himself fit for any Ecclesiastical Employment ; and therefore offer'd himself to be Try'd by the *Presbytery* of *Dalkeith*, who rejected him for Insufficiency, as some yet alive can Testifie to the *World.*

After this Repulse, he began to Project some other way of Living ; and was shortly after Recommended to the *Laird* of *Dundas*, to be Pedagogue to his Children, and Domestick Chaplain for saying *extemporary* Prayers. He passed some time in this Family for a Gifted and very Holy Young Man ; 'till some of the Servants observed an extraordinary Familiarity betwixt him and a Young Woman, who was the Old Gardiner's Wife. Being possess'd with this Suspicion, they observ'd him the more ; and one Night as they were

watch-

watching, they faw his *Miftrefs* go to his Chamber, which was a Summer-houfe built on the Garden-wall. The Key, as it happen'd, was left on the out-fide of the Door, which one of thofe that watched obferving, gently lock'd the Door upon them, and immediately ran to call his Mafter, who came to the Garden to fee what would be the Event. After they had been as long as they pleas'd together, at laft *Hortenfia* comes to go out ; who to her great Confufion finding the Door lock'd, fteps back to the *Adulterer* ; who, fearing that fhe fhould be taken with him, immediately let her down the Garden-wall, by the help of his Shirt, fhe hanging at one end, and he holding the other as naked as when he was Born. His Patron all this while beheld him like a filthy 𝕻𝖗𝖎𝖆𝖕𝖚𝖘 upon the Garden-wall, and the next Day in great Indignation difcharged him of his Service and Houfe. I fuppofe this is one of his particular and private Sins, which you'll find him hereafter confeffing in his Speech, deferved a worfe Death than he endured.

Afterwards he came to *Edinburgh*, where he liv'd fome Years in a Widow's Houfe, call'd Mrs. *Griffald Whitford*, who dwelt in the *Cow-gate* ; and with whom that Difhonour of Mankind, Major *Weir* was Boarded at the fame time. By his Converfation, it may be prefumed, that *Mitchel* improved much in the Art of Hypocrifie, and Drank in more deeply thofe Murderous and Treafonable Principles, which he afterwards practifed in the whole Courfe of his Life, and juftified at his Death. Now began he to Converfe with the moft Bigot Zealots againft Authority, to frequent and hold Conventicles to Preach up the Covenant, and to the utmoft of his Power to promote the Schifm, which was begun in the Church. By thefe Practices, he much endear'd himfelf to his Tutor Major *Weir*, who recommended him for a Chaplain to a *Fanatical* Family, the Lady whereof was Niece to Sir *Archibald Johnfton* Laird of *Warefton*, one of the moft furious Rebels againft the late Bleffed *KING*, and greateft Compliers with the lateUfurpation in theThree Kingdoms ; and whom you may remember to have been *Prefident of the Committee of Safety:* For all which accumula-ted Treafons he was Executed here in 1663.

During his Abode in this Family, broke out the Rebel-lion of the *Fanaticks* in 1666. He no fooner heard of it, but joyned with the Rebels, who were defeated at *Pentland-bills* : Though Mr. *Welfh* (as it is reported) during the Fight, prayed with up-lifted Hands to the Lord of Hofts againft *Amalek* (as his Spirit moved him to Mif-call the Royal Forces) and had his Hands ftayed up by fome of
his

his Brethren, as *Moses* had his by *Aaron* and *Hur*. Mr.
Mitchel had the Fortune to Escape from the Field, but was
afterwards Proclaimed Traytor, with many other Principal
Actors in the Rebellion; and afterwards excepted by Name
in his Majesty's Gracious Proclamation of Pardon, that he
might receive no Benefit thereby. From this time he
skulk'd about, and shelter'd himself among the Rebellious
Saints of the Brotherhood, till the Devil tempted him to
Assassin the Lord *Primate*, for which he hath Expiated by
his Blood.

Among others of his Excellent Qualifications, I have told
you what an utter *Ignoramus* he was: And I cannot forbear
to tell you farther, that *Welsh* and *Arnot*, and all the rest
of them are full as Illiterate as he; and that their insuperable
Ignorance in Divine and Humane Learning, is the Mother
of their Murdering Zeal. Indeed all the late Troubles
upon the Account of *Episcopacy*, are chiefly to be ascribed
to the shameful Ignorance of *Protestant* Divines in Ecclesiastical Antiquity; who looking no farther back into the
History of Religion, than the time of the *Reformation*,
and some of them not so far, did either hate Episcopacy as
an Usurpation, or else looked upon it as a meer Human
Constitution; and so could not have that particular Veneration for it, that was due to an Apostolical Ordinance, so
visibly founded in the Scriptures, and which was the sole
invariable Government of GOD's Universal Church for
above 1500 Years.

Of this, that excellent Man, Mr. *Henderson* was a de-
plorable Example; who tho' he was a Man of great Temper
and Prudence, and very Learned in his way; yet want of
Antiquity, of which he was ignorant, was the unhappy
Cause, why he engaged for the *Covenant* against the King,
and the Church. Had he spent but half so many Hours in that,
he had never moved so excentrically to the Church, nor done
those things; for which he expiated with Tears before his
late Blessed Majesty at *Newcastle*; afterwards spending the
short Remainder of his Life, in a sorrowful Penitential Retirement; for which he grew suspected by his Brethren of
the Covenant, who called him Apostate from the Cause.
There are many Persons yet alive, who can Testifie this to
be true; which may Teach all Divines, how dangerous it
is for them to Live in Ignorance of Ecclesiastical Antiquity,
which is so easily acquir'd, and so useful to be known. That
comprehensive Genius, Mr. *Calvin*, wanted nothing but this
to make him as Orthodox, and Consummate a Divine, as
ever was in the Church of GOD: For had he been but

C   half

half as well verſed in the more Primitive Eccleſiaſtical
Writers, as he was in St. *Auguſtine*, he had never Coin'd
the Notion of a Lay-Elder, defended the *Horrible Decree*,
or been expoſed for ſo many Abſurdities by meek * *Caſſander's*
Pen.

But to Conclude this Digreſſion with Mr. *Henderſon*,
there were very few, among our Covenanting-Miniſters,
Comparable to him for Prudence and Learning; and yet
even the lower moſt Form of our former *Presbyterians* were
great Men in compariſon to theſe of the *Remonſtrator Faction*,
who are all burning Zeal, but no Knowledge; as you will
perceive, not only by the Sequel of this Story, but this Letter of an ignorant Miniſter, that lately Revolted from our
Church.

S I R,

*I Received your Letter of the 15th of July, wherein you ſay,
That on the firſt Wedneſday of* Auguſt, *you are to have a
Presbytery, (you ought to have term'd it a Meeting of the Ex-
erciſe) and on the ſecond* Wedneſday *of* Auguſt, *a Provincial
Meeting with your Biſhop of* Rotheſay. *And once for all I
deſire you may take this for an abſolute Anſwer. Firſt, That
G O D hath for a long time been dealing with my Conſcience,
but eſpecially ſince* October laſt, *when I was called to* Mul *for
Electing Mr.* Andrew Wood, *Biſhop (I confeſs his want of the
Iriſh Language did ſtick with me, beſides many other things as
well now as before, about the Election of Mr.* James Ramſey;
*and all of you, ſave one, did then profeſs, that they did ſtick
with you alſo, though now you have ſwallowed down that Pill
with many more) and that in ſuch an extraordinary dreadful,
and terrible Manner, for my engaging to Prelacy, and a Lordly
Government over the Church of Chriſt (contrary to which there
lie ſo many Ties, and Obligations on this Land) that, with the
Grace of God, I would not adventure to abide the Terror of the
Lord for all the Stipends and Preferments in* Europe. *And
truly the worſt I wiſh to you, or any Prelate in* Britain *or*
Ireland, *or their Adherents, is, That they may have as ſound
a yoaking with their Conſciences, as I have had; if they be not
incorrigible Enemies of* Chriſt. *Next, Upon ſerious ſearch of
the Word of* GOD, *and of* Antiquity, *I am the more confirmed
in my Reſolution.* Blondellus, Salmatius, Gerſon, Bucer,
yea the whole current of Primitive Fathers, eſpecially
Smectymnuus, *have vindicated Presbytery againſt the whole*

* *In defenſ. lib. de Offic. Pii viri.*

World. I want not many more solid Reasons to add, only I suppose I could never be satisfied in them, and therefore I forbear.

To Conclude, I do here before GOD, and the whole World profess my disowning of Lordly Prelacy, as it is now Establish'd in our Land, which I was once most fully engaged into; and my firm and resolute Adherence to the Doctrine, Worship, Discipline, and Government of Scotland, as it was professed in this Nation, from the Year of our Lord 205. and downward for the space of 230 Years, and then since the Year 1580, till the Year 1610. and then from the Year 1638, till the Year 1661. and from thence downwards by many Godly in these three Lands, till this very Day is ; and more particularly to the Point, that Government of Christ's Church by an Equality and Parity of Pastors and Minister, all of them with one Shoulder carrying on the Work of the Lord, and exercising the Keys of Order and Jurisdiction, Doctrine and Discipline In Communi, according to due Order, and feeding the Flock of GOD ; not as being Lords of GOD's Heritage, but Ensamples to the Flock ; Yea, I do here (with all the Lord's faithful Servants and Witnesses in these three Lands, both in the present, and some former Generations, and with all the Lords Witnessing, and Suffering Servants and People, that have been, or now are in this Land, or present Generation) confess and bear my Witness and Testimony, the Cause of God, and the Work of Reformation, so much as was attained thereof, how afflicted and born down soever, and to the Confessions of Faith of the Church of Scotland, and of the three Kingdoms ; and to rational, and trinational Covenant ; and that I do rather choose to suffer Affliction with the poor suffering People of GOD, than to enjoy the Pleasures of Sin for a Season ; esteeming the Reproaches for Christ greater Riches than all the Pleasures and Preferments in the World. I desire you, with your Brethren, to consider those Scriptures, and take them home to you ; Isa. 66. 5. Zach. 11. 5, John 16. 2, 3. John 9. 1, 10. Remember your worthy Bedfellow, that is this Day, I hope, in Glory, shall bear Witness against you. Farewel for ever, Lordly Prelacy, for I had never a joyful Hour since I engaged therein ; and welcome, welcome my dear Lord Jesus Christ, I Embrace thee with the Arms of my Soul, and thy Cross ; I profess this, confess thee bearing my Testimony to thee, and thy persecuted Truth ; and by thy Blood, and the Word of thy Testimony ; and not loving my Life unto the Death, I hope to overcome.

Cambre-Me,   Sic Subscribit, Alex. Symer, Minister
August 6, 1677.   of the Gospel at Cambre.

Un e&s;

Unless you are vers'd in our Historian *Buchanan*, you will wonder, why this Learned Antiquarian should assert, That the Government of our Church was *Presbyterian* from the first Plantation of the Gospel in 205, or rather 203, till the Arrival of *Palladius* in the middle of the Fifth Century: You must know therefore, That all the Authority our *Presbyterians* have for this Assertion, is from *Buchanan*, that furious Enemy of Bishops; who in the Fifth Book of his History, writes, that the Church in the aforesaid time was not Govern'd by Bishops, but by the Monks or *Culdees*; which, were it true, as it is false, would prove, that the Government of the Church in that Interval, was not *Presbyterian*, but perfectly *Laical*, seeing it was long after that time, that Monks were admitted among the Clergy; and permitted to meddle with Church Affairs. But you may find a larger Confutation of this groundless Assertion of *Buchanan*, in Archbishop *Spotswood's* History.

But to continue my Narrative of Mr. *Mitchel*, I proceed to acquaint you with other memorable Things, that happened between his Condemnation and Execution, which was on *Friday* the 18th of *January*, in the Grass-Market, about three of the Clock in the Afternoon.

Some time before the Execution, the Reverend Mr. *Annand*, Dean of *Edinburgh*, not discourag'd with the unthankful Returns one of his Brethren had receiv'd from the Malefactor before, out of his tender Compassion to his Soul, wrote him a very affectionate and pious Letter, wherein he endeavour'd to shew him from the Gospel, how contrary his Principles and Practices were to the Doctrine of Christianity; and Exhorted him to Repentance for that Un-christian Attempt, by which he design'd to take away the Life of one Sacred Person, and grievously wounded another, &c. To all which, he returned this Answer.

SIR,

I *Received yours, and since my time is very short, and so very precious, I can only thank you for your Civility and Affection, whether real or pretended; and I tell you, I truly close with all the Precepts of the Gospel to Love and Peace; and therefore pray I both for Mr.* Sharp, *and you. But knowing both Mr.* Sharp's *Wickedness, and my own Sincerity; and the Lord's Holy Sovereignty, to use his Creatures as he pleases; I can only refer the Manifestation of my Fact, to the Day of* G O D's *Righteous and Universal Judgment; praying heartily, that* G O D *may have*

have Mercy on you, and open your Eyes to see both the Wickedness of all your Ways, and of your godless insulting over an unjustly condemned dying Man; and grant unto you Repentance and Remission of your Sins. I am in this your Well-wisher;

James Mitchel

The Dean in his Letter, urged an excellent Argument to Convince him, That the Impulse, which was upon him so many Years to Assassin the Primate, could not come from GOD, like the Impulse of Phineas, and the Zealots; because he fail'd in the Attempt; which never any Person did or could do, that was moved by GOD to do an Heroick Act. But, you see, the blind Pseudo-Zealot takes no notice of this Argument in his Answer; wherein to shew what an implacable Enemy he was to the Office, as well as the Person of the Archbishop, he mentions his Grace not by his Character, but by his Name.

Having been told in the Prison, That he would not be permitted to speak to the People before his Execution, he transcribed several Copies of his intended Speech; whereof one was found in his Pocket, and taken from him before he was carried out to Execution. It is long, and the former Part containing nothing but Libellous Reflections on the Privy-Council, the Judges, and the King's Advocate; I shall content my self to send you a Transcript of the latter.

I Acknowledge my particular and private Sins have been such, as have Merited a worse Death unto me; but I Die in the Hope of the Merits of Jesus Christ, to be freed from those eternal Punishments due to me for Sin. Yet I am confident, that GOD doth not plead with me in this Place, for my private and particular Sins; but that I am brought here, that the Work of GOD might be made Manifest; and for the Tryal of Faith, John 9. 3. 1 Pet. 1. 7. And that I may be a Witness for his despised Truth, and Interest in this Land, who am called to Seal the same with my Blood. And I wish heartily, that this my poor Life may put an End to the Persecution of the true Members of Christ in this Kingdom, so much adware by these perfidious Prelates; and in Opposition to whom, and in Testimony of the Cause of Christ, I at this time willingly lay down my Life; and bless my GOD that he hath thought me so much worthy to do the same for his Glory and his Rest. concerning a Christian Duty in a singular

my particular Judgment, concerning both Church and State; as is evidently Declar'd, and Manifested more fully else-where. So farewell all Earthly Enjoyments, and welcome Father, Son and Holy Spirit, into whose Hands I commend my Spirit.

As to that particular Christian Duty in an extraordinary Case, and his Judgment concerning Church and State, manifested; he means a larger blasphemous Libel, which he left behind him, wherein he endeavours to justifie his Fact. It is very long, but yet I beseech you to read it over; and if you have not read *Naphthali*, nor *Jus Populi vindicatum*, which is a Reply to the Answer, which the Bishop of *Orkney*, whom this Miscreant wounded, made to *Naphthali*; I am confident, you must be surpriz'd with Horror and Astonishment, to see such Unchristian Doctrines come from a Christian Pen. Yet the Primitive Churches never receiv'd the Apostolick Epistles with greater Veneration, than the Members of our Field-Congregations receive such Discourses as this; nor can any Church-man respect any Ancient Ecclesiastical Writer half so much as they adore *Naphthali*, which is written in the Defence of the Rebellion in 1666. and wherein this horrid Man's attempt upon the Primate is commended for an *Heroical Act*; and that cursed Book, with *Lex, Rex, Jus Populi vindicatum* and *Mr. Rutherford's Letters*, are the Fathers and Counsels of our *Fife*, and *Western Whigs*.

I have here subjoyn'd the Account of my Self, Principles and foresaid Practices, as they were set down in a Letter to a Friend; and another Declaration both written by me, when first Convened before the Lords Justices, in the Year 1674.

The Copy of my Letter, *Edinburgh-Tolbooth*, *February* the 16th, 1674.

SIR,

ME (who may justly call my Self the least of all Saints, and the chiefest of all Sinners) hath Christ his Son our Lord called, to be a Witness for his destroyed Truth and trampled on Interest, by this Wicked, Blasphemous and God-contemning Generation, and against all their other perfidious Wickedness.

Sir,

Sir, I say, the confidence I have in your real friendship; but Love
to Christ, his Truth, People, Interest and Cause, hath encouraged
me to write to you, hoping that you will not mis-construct, nor
take advantage of my Infirmities and Weakness. The have
heard of my Indictment, which I take up in these two Particulars: First, (as they term it) Rebellion and Treason, anent
which I answer'd to my Lord Chancellor, That it was no Rebellion, but a Duty which every one was bound to have performed, in joining with that Party. And in the Year 1656,
Mr. Robert Lightonne, being the Primate of the College of
Edinburgh before our Laureation, tendered to us the National
Covenant, and Solemn League and Covenant; which upon
mature Deliberation, I found nothing in them, but a short
Compend of the Moral Law only; obliging us to our Duty
towards G O D, and Men in their several Stations; and I
finding, that our then Banished King's Interest lay wholly in-
cluded therein, Viz. Both the Oath of Coronation, Allegiance,
&c. And they being the then Testers of all Loyalty. And, my
Lord, it was well known, that then many were taking the
Tender, and for-swearing Charles Stuart's Parliaments and
House of Lords, I then subscribed them both. The doing of
which, my Lord Chancellor, would have stood me at no less rate,
if all's well known, than this my present adhering and prosecuting the Ends thereof, doth now: And when I was Question'd,
What then I called Rebellion; I Answer'd, That it is (Exro 7.
26,) And whosoever will not do the Law of thy God, and
of the King, &c. But being Question'd by the Commissioner,
before the Council there anent; I Answered, as I said to my
Lord Chancellor before, in the Year 1656. Mr. Robert
Lightonne being then Primate of the College of Edinburgh,
before our Laureation, he tendered to us the National Covenant,
and solemn League and Covenant; where he stopp'd me, saying,
I made you are come here to give a Testimony: And then being
demanded, what I called Rebellion, if it was not Rebellion to
oppose his Majesty's Forces in the Face? To which I Answer'd,
My Lord Commissioner, if it please your Grace, I humbly con-
ceive, that they should have been with us; meaning that it was
the Duty of those Forces to have joined with us, according to the
National Covenant; at which Answer I perceiv'd him to storm.
But, says he, I hear that you have been over Seas, with whom
did you Converse there? Answer, With my Merchant, my
Lord. But saith he, with whom in particular? With one
John Mitchel, a Cousin of mine. Saith he, I have heard well
of him, he is a Factor in Rotterdam; to which I conceded.
But saith he, did you not Converse with Mr. Lovingston, and
such as he? To which I Answered, my Lord Commissioner, I

con-

concerned with our banish'd *Ministers*? To which he Reply'd,
banish'd *Ministers*! banish'd. *Traytors*! He will speak Treason
at the very Bar. Then he answered himself, saying, But they
would all the *Shooting* at the *Bishop*, an Heroick Act? To which
I Answered, That I never told them of any such thing. Question,
But where did you see James Wallace last? Answ. Towards
the Borders of *Germany*, some Years ago. Quest. But what
asked you at my Lord St. Andrews here? pointing at him with
his Finger. Answ. My Lord Commissioner, the grievous
Oppression and horrid Bloodshed of my Brethren, and the
eager Pursuit after my own Blood, as it appeareth this
Day to your Grace, and to all his Majesty's Honourable
Council: After which he commanded to take me away,
that they might see next what to do with me.

The Second is, The *Shooting* that Shot, intended against the
Bishop of St. Andrews, whereby the *Bishop* of Orkney was
hurt; to which I Answer'd my Lord Chancellor in private,
Viz, That I looked upon him to be the main Instigator of all
the Oppression and Bloodshed of my Brethren, that followed
thereupon; and the continued pursuing after my own: And my
Lord Chancellor, as it was credibly reported to us (the Truth of
which your Lordship knows better than we) that he kept up his
Majesty's Letter, inhibiting any more Blood to be shed upon that
Account, until the last Ten were Executed; and I being a
Soldier, not having laid down Arms, but being still upon my
own Defence, nor having any other Quarrel nor Aim at any
Man, but according to my own Apprehension of him, and that, as
I hope, in Sincerity, without fixing either my self or any one
upon the Covenant, it self, and as it may be understood, by
many thousands of the Faithful; besides the prosecuting of the
Ends of the same Covenant, which was, and is in that Part
the Overthrow of Prelates and Prelacy: And I being a declar'd
Enemy to him upon that Account, and he to me in like manner; so I never found my self oblig'd, either by the Law of
GOD, or Nature, to set a Sentry at his Door for his Safety;
But as he was always ready to take his Advantage of me, as it
now appeareth, so I of him when Opportunity offer'd: Moreover,
we being in no term of Capitulation, but on the contrary, I by
his Instigation being excluded from all Grace and Favour,
thought it my Duty to pursue him upon all Occasions. Also, my
Lord, Sir William Sharp making his Apology anent his un-
handsome cheating way, when he took me under pretext to have
spoken with me, about some other Matter (I not knowing him
until Five or Six of his Brothers, and his own Servants were
laying fast hold on me, they being armed of purpose) he desired
that I would excuse him, seeing what he had done was upon his

Bre-

Brothers Account; which *Excuse*, my *Lord*, I *easily admitted* of, *feeing that he thought himfelf obliged to do what he did without Law or Order, in the behalf of his Brother; much more was* I *obliged to do what I did, in behalf of many Brethren, whofe Oppreffion was fo great, and whofe Blood he had caufed fhed in fuch abundance:* Moreover, *he infifting in his bloody Murders, as witnefs the wounding Mr.* Bruce *at his taking of his Emiffaries, fome few Days before that fell out concerning himfelf* ; now, *If by any means in taking him away, I could have put a ftop to the then current Perfecution:* *Thus far I have truly refumed what paft.*

But this *Anfwer to the fecond Part of the Indictment, may be thought by fome to be a ftep out of the ordinary way* ; where-*fore I fhall offer thefe things following to your Confideration,* viz. *That paffage,* Deut. 13. 9. *Where to me it is manifeft, That the* Seducer *or* Inticer to *Worfhip* falfe Gods, *is to be put to Death by the Hands of thofe whom he feeketh to turn away from the* Lord, *efpecially by the Hand of the Witneffes, whereof I am one* ; *as it appears* Deut. 13. 9. *which Precept I humbly conceive to be Moral, and not meerly Judicial, and that it is not at all* *Ceremonial* or Levitical: *But as every Moral Precept is Uni-verfal as to the Extent of Place, fo alfo as to the Extent of Time and Perfons* ; *upon which Command, Sir, I do really think that* Phineas *acted in taking away the* Midianitifh *Whore, and him whom fhe had feduced,* Numb. 25. 6. *Alfo that* Elijah *by vertue of that Precept, gave Commandment to the People to deftroy* Baal's *Priefts, contrary to the Mind of the feducing Magiftrate, who was not only remifs and negligent in executing Juftice, but became a Protector and Defender of the Seducers:* *Then and in that Cafe, I fuppofe the Chriftian's Duty not to be very dark. Moreover. we fee what the People of* Ifrael *did,* 2 Chron. 31. 1. *They deftroyed Idolatry, not only in* Judah, *where the King concurred, but in* Ephraim *and* Manaffeh, *where the King himfelf was an Idolater* ; *and furely what all the People were bound to do, as their Duty by the Law of* GOD, *every one was bound to do it to the uttermoft of their Power and Capacity.* And as it is, Ezek. 13. 3. *Where the Seducer's Father and Mother fhall put him to Death* ; *I take this to be meant of the Chriftian Magiftrate. But when he is withdrawn by the feducer from the Exercife of his Office and Duty, and he's become utterly Remifs and Negligent in putting the Seducer to Death, according to* GOD's *exprefs Law* ; *which is not to be expected of him (for then he fhould do Juftice upon himfelf) but is become a Protector and Defender of the Idolater* ; *then I doubt not, but it doth become the Duty of every Chriftian, to the uttermoft of his Power and Capacity, to deftroy and cut off both,*

both, *Idolatry* and *Idolaters*. *Yea, these presumptuously-mur-*
thering Prelates ought to be kill'd by the Avenger of Blood,
when he meeteth them, by the express Law of GOD; seeing
the thing is manifestly true, Numb. 25. 21. *and not have*
liberty to flee to such Cities of Refuge, as the vain Pretext of
Lawful Authority: But they should be taken even from the
Horns of such Altars, and be put to Death. Moreover, what
is spoken of concerning Amalek, *upon the account, that he de-*
sign'd and resolv'd the Extirpation of the Lord's People and Truth,
who are his Throne, upon which he puts forth his Hand; and
because he took occasion against them, Exod. 17. 15. Numb.
24. 20. *He endeavouring that GOD should not have a*
People to have served him, according to his revealed Will, upon
the Earth; and if he could have effected his Design, they should
not have lived, who would not serve and worship him, and his
Idol-Gods: And for the better effectuating this his Design, he
took occasion against them when they were weary, in coming
out of Egypt, Deut. 25. 17, 18. *And the reason there*
annexed, is, That he feared not GOD. Now, because I know
Bishops *both will, and do say, That what they did against those*
of the Lord's People, whom they Murdered, they did by Law
and Authority, but what I did, was contrary to both: Answ.
The King himself, and all the Estates of the Land, and every
individual Person therein, both were, and are obliged, by the
Oath of GOD upon them, to have by force of Arms, extir-
pated perjured Prelates and Prelacy; and in doing thereof, to
have defended one another with their Lives and Fortunes; the
Covenants being engaged into, upon these Terms, Viz. *After*
Supplications, Remonstrations, Protestations, and all other
lawful Means have been used; now for that effect, as the last Re-
medy, we take up Arms; upon which Conditions, the Nobility,
and all the Representatives of the Nation, according to the
National, and Solemn League and Covenant, gave to our King
both the Sword and Scepter, and set the Crown upon his Head;
and he accordingly received them, according to these Sacred
Oaths and Promises, and swore by the Ever-living GOD, to
use and improve them for the End aforesaid; and especially, in
order to the performing of this Article, Viz. *The Extirpation*
and Over-throw of Prelates and Prelacy: And now the want
of what Authority do they mean or speak of? Truly I know not,
except it be the Authority of their Aggregation of new Gods,
of whom they have their Gain, Life and Standing, Viz.
Chemosh *or* Bacchus, *which with drunken* Moab, *delighted*
to dwell within dark Cells. and Ashteroth *and* Venus, *whom*
they worship in the Female-kind, because of their Adulteries
and Whoredoms; as also Milchom *or* Molech, *which signifies*
a Ty-

a Tyrannical King, or a Devil, if they will have it so.; in
whose Arms and Power they put their young Infants and
Posterity to be Burnt and Destroyed, according to his Lust and
Pleasure, Amos 5. 26. Psalm 116. 37. and that Mammon,
which they delight to worship daily, together with their own
Bellies, whose glory is their shame; who mind Earthly things;
whose End will be Destruction, except they repent, which there
is little probability of, Psalm 3. 19. To which if we may
add their abominable Pride, and Blasphemous Perjury, then
their Gods will be equal in number to the Whore their Mother, from whom they have their being, strength and standing;
and from the Devil their Father, who was a Deceiver, Lyar,
Murderer from the beginning : And now seeing the Prelates
possess whatsoever their Gods, Chemosh, &c. giveth them to
possess, then why should not we possess what the Lord our God
giveth us to possess, viz. His eternal Truths manifested to us,
in his revealed Will, and keep and defend the same, from all In-
novations, Corruptions and Traditions of his or our Adversaries,
defend our Lives, Laws and Liberties out of the Hands of our
Usurping Enemies, Jude 11. 24. for sure I am, that God once
dispossest the Prelates and Malignants of all these, and should
they again possess through our defect, God forbid. But the like
of this work, our Murthering Prelates like not; who plead like
the Whore their Mother for passive Obedience; and that all the
Lords People, who may not comply with your Idolatries, should
lay down their Necks to their bloody Axes; with whom too too
many of our Hypocritical time-serving and perfidious Professors
do agree, who would rather abide with Reuben, amongst the
Sheep-folds, than Jeopard either life or fortune in the help of the
Lord against the Mighty, but do not consider the bitter Curse
pronounced by the Angel of the Lord against Meroz; to which
he immediately subjoins a Blessing upon Jael, the Wife of Hebar
the Kenite: Others excuse themselves thus, viz. Vengeance is
mine, and I will re-pay; but so the Throne and Judgment is the
Lord's; and by this they would take away the Use and Office of
Magistracy, which erroneous Principle I detest; for G O D even
in the working of Miracles, viz. in dividing the Red Sea,
Exod. 14. 16. he commanded Moses to stretch forth his Rod;
and Christ, when he opened the blind Man's Eyes, maketh use
of Clay and of Spittle; tho' indeed, I mean not of any who were
willing to have helped, but wanted opportunity; yet there are
many peevish time-serving Professors, who resolve they shall never
suffer so long as they have either Soul or Conscience to Morgage;
providing that they may save them from Suffering; and if it
will not do their Business, it seemeth (that before they suffer)
they resolve to sell out at the ground. Now, Sir, I have neither

mist

mis-interpreted Scripture, nor mis-apply'd it, in regard of the Persons here hinted at, nor been wrong in the End, which ought to be the Glory of GOD, and the good of his Church and People. Then I think that some Persons might forbear to scourge me so sore with their Tongues, while I am not yet Condemned by the common Enemy; and my bearing of some things, reported by some behind my Back, hath occasion'd my writing to you at this time. O Sir, be intreated to pray to the Lord in my behalf, that he would be pleased out of his Mercy and Goodness, to save me from Sinning under Suffering, in this Hour and Power of Darkness; for my Soul is prest in me, in the search betwixt Sin and Duty, viz. lest I should be too niggard and sparing of Life, when GOD calleth for it; and upon the other Hand, lest I should be too prodigal and lavish of it, in not using all legal Defences in preserving of it; and many things of the like Nature. I am in a strait, O Lord, undertake thou for me. Sir, I hope you will excuse me, in sending you these indistinct and irregular Lines, when you consider my present condition. Sir, believe, I would many times, when I am before them, think a Scaffold a sweet Retirement, lest they should cheat and deceive me; in making me, either to stain the declarative Glory of GOD, my own Conscience, or his People and Interest, in wronging of them, either by opening of the Adversaries Mouths against them, or in letting loose their Hand upon them: Henceforth let the Adversary either say or do what they can, yet the Righteous will hold on their way, and he who hath clean Hands will be stronger and stronger, *Job* 17. 9. But he that saith unto the Wicked, Thou art Righteous, him shall the People Curse, Nations shall abhor him, *Prov.* 24. 24. Farewell in the Lord.

P. S. It is acknowledged by all Rational Royalists, That it is Lawful for any private Person to kill an Usurper, or Tyrant, *sine titulo*; and to kill *Irish* Robbers and Tories, or the like; and to kill Boars, Wolves, and such Devouring Beasts; because the good of this Action doth not redound to the Person himself only, but to the whole Commonwealth; and the Person Acting incurs the Danger himself alone. The Second Part of *The Cloud of Witnesses*, P. 60. Mr. *Knox*, has these express Words, For GOD, saith he, had not only given me Knowledge and a Tongue, to make known the impiety of the Idol, but had given me Credit with many, who would have put in Execution GOD's Judgments, if I would only have consented thereto. But so careful was I of common Tranquility, and so loth was I to offend some, that in secret Conference with Zealous Men, I Travell'd

rather

rather to flacken that Fervency, GOD had kindled in them, than to animate or encourage them, to put their Hands to the Lord's Work; wherein I acknowledge my felf to have done moft wickedly ; and from the bottom of my Heart I do ask my GOD pardon, that I did not what in me lay, to have fuppreft that Idol in the Beginning. But, O! How far are the Men in our Time from fuch Convictions, whofe Work it is to put out any Spark of Life or Zeal, which appeareth in any Perfon, againft Idolatry, and Idol of our times. Now let Men, whether Foes or Friends, Carp or Quarrel never fo much, yet the Purpofe and Determination of GOD will not be difappointed, in living Witneffes arainft this mif-believing Generation, *Viz.* That he is both All-powerful and Willing to Deliver one or more of his People trufting in Him : Yea, and that *there is no reftraint unto the Lord, to fave by many or by few,* 1 Sam. 14. 6. If any be Obedient to the Voice of his Commandments, altho' Succefs doth not always follow thereupon, more than it did to *Ifrael,* Jofh. 7. 12. againft the City of *Ai,* becaufe there was an *Achan* in the Camp; and, alas, there are many *Achans* in the Camp of our *Ifrael,* which caufe the Lord's People to fall Daily before their Enemies ; and which makes all their Endeavours unfuccefsful : I mean, the hidden time-ferving Hypocrites and Mumurers, who have preferred their Backs and Bellies to the Intereft of GOD, and their Hearts ftill defirous to return to *Ægypt.* I fay, until fuch Rebels be Purged, and Dye, we can have little expectation to Profper in any Enterprize or Undertaking ; for they have both Betray'd and Mif-believed GOD, notwithftanding of all his Miracles which he did of Old, and which he has done in our Days, for his People, and before their Eyes ; yet they are fo far gone back in a Courfe of Apoftacy and Com-pliance with the *Canaanites* of our Times, and are become fo brutifhly Ignorant of the exprefs Law of GOD, and are fuch Enemies thereto, that they do rather concur with the faid *Canaanites,* Judg. 6. 25. to have *Gideon* put to Death for performing his Duty, conform to the exprefs Com-mand of GOD, than either to Study thereof themfelves, or give Obedience thereto. But if it be Objected, that. *Gideon* had an exprefs Command from GOD, for throwing down of *Baal's* Altar, and for cutting down of the Grove, and deftroying of the *Midianites. Anfwer,* Indeed he had an exprefs Command of GOD for his Encouragement ; but he had no new Command from GOD, fave that which, was exprefly enjoined upon all the *Ifraelites;* by virtue of which, every one was obliged to have done what he did, with-

without any such Message from GOD, *Deut.* 7. 2, 3, 15. and who are readier with *Judas* (before they incur danger or loss) to send three thousand Men to bring *Sampson* bound to the *Philistines*, than to have sent him ten of his Assistance against the common Enemy; concerning the Truth of which, we have gotten many sad Experiments. But however, I hope, that what hath been said, shall occasion a further Cognition of, and a more serious Search into these fore-mentioned Truths, than hath been for a long Time by-past.

That, albeit I have singly Declared my own Motives and Reasons for that Attempt and Shooting; wherein I then had, and now have Peace, and Hope to find Acceptance of GOD, according to the Multitude of his Mercies, to such as Seek and Fear him in Sincerity: Yet, I will not take on me. Absolutely, and in every Respect, to Justifie or Assert, That it is my own deliberate and fixed Principle; let be that it is justfied by, and is the Principle of the *Nonconforming Presbyterian Party* of the Church of *Scotland*; of which I have the Honour and Happiness to be one, the unworthiest of many: Nay, if I should say so of them, I would be found a Lyar against the Truth; for I adventur'd on it upon my own pure and proper Motion, without the Instigation of any, yea, without the Privacy of that Party; whom therefore I earnestly desire, that none may Charge with; and if any shall, I do with the greatest Confidence aver, That they deal with them most unjustly. I have, I say again, in the Simplicity of my Heart, with Candour and Ingenuity, becoming a Dying Man, and a Christian, believing that he must be made Manifest before the Tribunal of Christ, and there receive according to the Things done in the Body, whether they be Good or Evil; giving an Account of the Reasons and Motives, pussing and pressing me on to it, wherein I had quietness of Mind in the Time, and have still to this present hour; hoping, that as he is Sovereign Lord over all Creatures, and may use any of them as Instruments to whatsoever his Pleasure is; and that, as I say, I did take, and do still look upon the Motion as from himself; so he will accept of my Sincerity in it; and one Day, both bring forth his own and my Righteousness as the Light,

His

His SPEECH at the Place of *Execution*.

'I Suppofe, fome will be defirous to know what hath
' brought me to this Place of Suffering ; to which I have
' no other Anfwer than that which *Elijah* gave, when
' threatned with Death by *Jezabel*, 1 *King* 19. 14. I have
' been very jealous for the Lord God of Hofts, becaufe
' the Children of *Ifrael* have forfaken thy Covenant,
' thrown down thine Altars and true Worfhip, and flain his
' Prophets and Minifters : And they feek my Life to take
' it away.

' With all my Heart and Soul, I own and adhere to the
' Work of Reformation, as it was begun and carried on in
' this Kingdom, according to the Word of GOD, and the
' National Covenant, and the Solemn League and Covenant ;
' as it was fettled amongft us in Doctrine, Worfhip, Difci-
' pline and Government, by general Affemblies, Synods,
' Presbyteries, Kirk-Seffions, and the Peoples juft Power
' to choofe and call their own lawful Paftors ; and I do de-
' clare, that I judge Patronage to be a Popifh Right, and an
' Ufurpation in the Houfe of GOD.

' I do believe and am perfwaded, that Magiftracy is an
' Ordinance appointed of GOD, as well under the New
' Teftament as it was under the Old ; and that whofoever
' refifteth the Lawful Magiftrate in the exercife of his Lawful
' Power, refifteth the Ordinance and Appointment of
' GOD, *Rom.* 13. 3. *For he is God's Minifter to you for thy good,*
' and in doing good thou needs not be afraid of him, 1 *Pet.*
' 2. 12. We muft obey the lawful Magiftrate for Confcience
' fake, *Deut.* 17. 15, 16, 17. The lawful Magiftrate muft
' be a Man qualified according to GOD's Appointment,
' and not according to the Peoples Luft and Pleafure, left in
' the End he fhould prove to them a Prince of *Sodom*, and a
' Governour of *Gomorrah*, whom GOD in his Righteoufnefs
' fhould Appoint for their Judgment, and Eftablifh for their
' Correction : He muft be one of thy Brethren, and not
' the Face of a Stranger ; he muft not make himfelf ftrong
' by Multiplying of Horfes, to the End he may compel the
' Lord's People to Rebel againft the Lord's exprefs Com-
' mand ; nor *Jeroboam*-like, compel the People to any courfe
' of Apoftacy ; he muft not multiply Wives to himfelf, and
' much lefs Whores, nor Marry an Idolatrous Wife like
' *Jezabel*, 1 *Kings* 16. 31. Nor be Covetous in Multiplying
' t)

' to himſelf Silver or Gold ; he muſt be a diligent Student
' of the Law of the Lord all the Days of his Life, that he
' turn neither to the Right Hand, nor to the Left Hand
' therefrom, but muſt judge the People accordingly ; other-
' wiſe neither he nor his Children can expect to prolong
' their Days, 2 Sam. 23. 3. He muſt not be a Son of Belial
' without or above Order and Law, whom a Man cannot
' touch except he be fenced with Iron, for ſuch ſhall all be
' preſt away ; for (ſaith David) he that ruleth over Men
' muſt be juſt, ruling in the fear of the Lord, &c. But if a
' Man ſimulating himſelf to be thus qualified, and thereafter,
' when he had ſtrengthned himſelf upon the Throne, ſhall
' abjure and ſacrifice his Oath and Covenant, both to GOD
' and his Subjects, and ſhall tranſgreſs the Law and Com-
' mandment of the Lord, who hath given the Magiſtrate
' only one accumulative Power, to promove, protect and
' defend GOD's Laws, Truth and People, from being cor-
' rupted, violated or any ways damnified ; and for that
' End he hath received both his Place and his Power from
' GOD and Men, for he hath not received of the Lord an
' obſtructive, deſtructive or privative Power ; for (as has
' been ſaid) the People can give no Right nor Power to
' any Man, but what is according to GOD's Appointment,
' leſt they ſhould incur the ſad Challenge from GOD, Hoſea
' 8. 4. They have ſet up Kings, but not by me ; they have
' made Princes, but I knew it not. For in Chap. 10. v. 3. Iſrael
' there is brought in confeſſing their fault, and they deny'd
' they had a King, becauſe he was not ſuch as G O D had
' Appointed, and ſaid, What ſhould a King do to them'
' Seeing he had partly by Force, and partly by Fraud,
' withdrawn them from the Fear and Obedience which
' they ought to G O D, and to his Law ; and had ſeduced
' and compell'd them to Idolatry, and worſhipping of falſe
' Gods : And if the Magiſtrate being in Power, ſhall over-
' turn the Covenant-work of GOD, his Truth and Inter-
' eſts, the Fundamental and Municipal Laws of the Land ;
' and moreover by a ſetled Parliament, according to his own
' Mind, and for his own Uſe and Ends, they, as the Peoples
' Repreſentatives, do by Acts Reſciſſory reſcind all Acts of
' laudable lawful Parliaments, Committee of States or
' Councils ; wherein were contained or comprehended any
' mutual Bond, Obligation, Covenant or Contract betwixt
' the Prince or People, he having diveſted himſelf of any
' legal Right he could have or pretend over ſuch a People,
' and they being in Statu quo prius, and none having Right
' to Rule over them without their own Conſent ; it th-

' ; fore-

‘ afore-said Magistrate shall then again Usurp and Invade
‘ his Peoples Lives, Religions, Liberties and Laws, and
‘ make even simple supplicating of him, Crimes of Treason,
‘ contrary to the Dictates of Nature; and he by armed
‘ Emissaries, and by his Arbitrary Power, carried on by
‘ the Sword in their Hands, compel the Lord's People to
‘ relinquish and to forsake the true Religion and Worship
‘ of GOD, and make a surrender of both their Soul, Con-
‘ science, Lives, Laws, Liberties, and imbrace a false Re-
‘ ligion and Will-worship, and engage to Serve and Wor-
‘ ship false and idol Gods at his Pleasure: For thus all that
‘ is dear and near to a People being in the extremity of
‘ hazard; now it necessarily follow'd to be the Duty of such
‘ People, or any part of them, to take up Arms in Defence
‘ of their Lives, Laws, Religion and Liberties, and of
‘ their Posterity, that they may not be left in such an into-
‘ lerable Bondage; and as they would not be accounted
‘ guilty of bringing G O D's Wrath upon the whole Land,
‘ *Jer.* 22. 2, 3. *Hear the word of the Lord, O King of Judah,*
‘ &c. *Thou and thy Servants, and the People that enter in by*
‘ *these Gates, execute Judgment and Righteousness, and deliver*
‘ *the oppressed out of the hand of the oppressor,* Chap. 37. 2. *But*
‘ *neither he, nor the Servants, nor the People of the Land*
‘ *hearkned to the Prophet Jeremiah, until Wrath from the Lord*
‘ *consumed them all.* Now, had it not been the Peoples
‘ Duty, to have Executed Judgment and Righteousness, and
‘ to have deliver'd the Oppressed out of the Hands of the
‘ Oppressor; *Zedekiah* and his Servants (which I think was
‘ meaned by the Nobility and Princes) proving deficient, in
‘ order to the performing of their Duty, it necessarily fol-
‘ loweth to be the Peoples Duty; for if it had not been their
‘ Duty, it had not been their Sin to have omitted it; but
‘ here we see it is as well charged home to be the Peoples
‘ Sin, as to be the Sin of the King, or the Sin of his Nobles:
‘ But, say some, Who shall be Judge is such Cases? To which
‘ I Answer, That the Law of G O D is the only Supreme
‘ and Infallible Judge in all such Cases; for what other Judge
‘ is, when two Kings or Monarhs falleth out in War, neither
‘ of them being Subject to any other Judge. But some Pro-
‘ phane and Brutishly Ignorant Malignant, saith, That this
‘ or that ignorant Fellow or Hussy, take upon them to
‘ determine what the Law of GOD saith in such Cases: I
‘ Answer, neither this nor that ignorant Fellow or Hussy,
‘ nor yet this or that ignorant, prophane, wicked or per-
‘ fidious Prince or Princess, is capable to be Judge, *Deut.*
‘ 30. 11. *For this Commandment which I command thee this*

E ‘ *Day,*

' *Day, it is not hidden from thee, neither is it far off,* verſe 12.
' *It is not in Heaven, that thou ſhouldſt ſay, Who ſhall go up for*
' *us to Heaven and bring it to us, that we may hear it and do*
' *it,* &c. *neither is it beyond the Sea,* &c. *but the word is very*
' *near unto thee, in thy Mouth and in thy Heart that thou may'ſt*
' *do it:* And in this Caſe I do appeal to any Man of a ſober
' Wit and Judgment, ſeeing the *Secrets of the Lord are with*
' *them that fear him,* Pſalm 25. 14. *And ſeeing evil Men un-*
' *derſtand not Judgment, but they that ſeek the Lord underſtand*
' *all things,* Prov. 28. 5. *For they know not how to do Right,*
' *who ſtore up Robbery in their Palaces,* Amos 3. 10. who is
' moſt capable to judge, what the Law of G O D deter-
' mineth in all ſuch matters. *Artaxerxes,* a great Monarch,
' Commanded, *That whatſoever is Commanded of the God*
' *of Heaven, that it ſhould be diligently done, for the Houſe of*
' *the God of Heaven; for why ſhould there be Wrath upon the*
' *King and his Sons?* Ezra 7. 23. But O how many Men at
' this time of the Sons of *Beliah,* contrary to what is here
' ſpoken of, skrew up thoſe who are above them to ſo high
' a Pinacle, and an Illimitated and Arbitrary Power, far
' above what either the Law of GOD, or the Law of Na-
' ture will admit of, for this very End and Purpoſe, that
' they may glory in the Works of their own Hands; and
' that he whom they have thus ſet up, and to whom they
' have made a ſurrender of both Credit, Conſcience and
' common Honeſty, may return unto them a Power over
' others who are under them, by putting Swords in the
' Hands of bloody Cut-throats; who are raiſed and keep'd
' up for that effect, to keep and bring into an *Ægyptian*
' Bondage, the Perſons, Lives, Laws, Liberties, yea even
' the Souls and Conſciences of the Lord's People; the
' which Power, I declare to be Diabolical, Prophane and
' Blaſphemous; and *Pharoah*-like to ſay, *Who is the Lord that*
' *they ſhould obey him?* Exod. 5. 2. Now ſeeing both the
' Throne and the Judgment is the Lord's, then O bleſſed
' and happy Magiſtrate, who Ruleth and Governeth his
' Subjects, keeping in a ſtreight Line of Subordination to
' GOD's Law and Statutes, for in ſo doing, Who may ſay
' to him, what doſt thou? *Prov.* And O happy and bleſſed
' People thus Governed, *Deut.* 4. 8. *And what Nation is*
' *there ſo great, that hath Statutes and Judgments ſo Righteous,*
' *as all this Law which I ſet before you this day?* But O the
' Blaſphemous Perjuries and Wickedneſs of this Apoſtate
' Generation, whom no Bands, Obligations nor Covenants
' can bind, except theſe ſpoken in the 149 Pſal. 8. But ſhall
' they thus break the Covenant, and eſcape and be deliver'd?
                                                    ' *Ezek.*

'*Ezek.* 17. 15, 18. As if the Lord's Hand and Power
'could not reach them, to inflict just and due Punishment
'upon them which commit such things. I do detest and
' abhor that woful Indulgence and Incroachment, and Usur-
' pation on the Crown and Prerogatives Royal of our Lord
' Jesus Christ (at least in the Givers thereof) howbeit, I
' have very much Love, Charity, and Affection to many
' who have embraced the same : For I do really think, that
' they have been outwitted in that Matter, and have not
' wickedly departed from following the Lord.; yet I hope
' they shall get their Souls for a Prey in the Day of the Lord,
' altho' they may suffer loss, in building such Hay and
' Stubble upon the Rock Christ Jesus, when that their Work
' shall be burnt up by the Fire of his Jealousie.

' I protest before G O D, Angels and Men, against all
' these Acts of Parliament or Council, which are against
' and derogative to the Work of G O D and Reformation,
' and carrying on of the same, according as we are ingaged
' and sworn in these holy Bands of the National Covenant,
' and Solemn League and Covenant : I abhor the shedding
' of the Blood of the Lord's People, for their adhering to
' the same, and the Peoples guarding such in Prison-houses
' and at Scaffolds unto their Death ; whom both by the
' Oath of G O D upon them, and by the Eminent and
' Laudable Laws of the Land, and by the Law of Nature,
' they were obliged to have defended to the uttermost of
' their Lives and Fortunes ; it being most well known,
' that such as were put to Death, had committed no Crime,
' but on the contrary had performed a Duty, which they
' were as much obliged to have performed as these, if the
' Guarders had been as faithful to GOD and Man as the
' Pannels were.

' Likewise I protest against their Banishment, Imprison-
' ment, or Finings or Confinements, and against all the
' Hardships and Perplexities of whatsoever kind which they
' have been put to, through the Iniquity of the Times ; so
' that we may justly with our Predecessors say, That our
' Persecutors have devoured us, and have crushed us ; have
' emptied us, swallow'd us up like a Dragon, and have filled
' their Bellies with our Delicates, and have cast us out, *Jer.*
' 5, 34. For which Cause, G O D gave a Charge to pre-
' pare Instruments for the Over-throw and Destruction of
' such Persecutors, *ver.* 12. Because it was the Vengeance
' of the Lord and of his Temple ; so shall our Remnant,
' who outlive these Persecutors, say, *ver.* 35. The Violence
' done to me and my Flesh, be upon *Babylon,* and my Blood

' be upon the Inhabitants of *Chaldea* ; let Wrath from the
' Lord purfue them, for their Blood, and Violence in their
' Perfons and Eftates, and their Strength wherein they
' confide, and in their Friends and Favorites; who have
' confulted and contrived within their wicked Courfes. I
' hope the time is drawing Nigh, and that the Joints of
' their Loins is loofing, their Knees are beginning to fmite
' one againft another, *Dan.* 5. 6. and the Hand-writing
' begins to be pourtrayed upon the Wall, becaufe they have
' not confider'd what G O D did to their Predeceffors, for
' their Idolatrous Pride and Wickednefs; altho' they knew
' it, yet they are become more infolent in Idolatry and
' Wickednefs, and daring againft G O D, than ever their
' Forefathers prefumed to be, in medling with the Veffels
' and Materials of GOD's Houfe, and with the Crown and
' Kingly Office of Chrift Jefus ; and have appropiate them
' to their own Idolatrous Ends and Ufes, *ver.* 21, 22. There-
' fore, when the forbifh'd Sword of the Lord's Indignation
' and Juftice breaketh forth to devour, which it may do
' before the dark Night of thefe dreadful Difpenfations pafs
' over ; then fhall the time-ferving Hypocrites of this Ge-
' neration begin to their untimely Prayers, *viz.* Hills and
' Mountains fall upon them, to hide them from the Face of
' the Righteous Judge ; For who may abide the Day of his
' coming, for Executing of Vengeance on his Adverfaries?
' In that Day the Man fhall be accufed who keepeth back his
' Sword from Blood, and who doth the Work of the Lord
' deceitfully, *Jer.* 48. 10. Yea, happy fhall he be, that taketh
' this curfed Malignant, and Prelatical Brood, and dafheth
' them againft the Stones ; yea, happy fhall he be, that reward-
' eth them as they have ferved us, *Pfalm* 137. For this
' honour have all his Saints, the high Praifes of G O D in
' ther Mouth, and a two Edged Sword in their Hand, to
' execute Vengeance upon the Heathen, *Pfalm* 149.

' Having thus deliver'd my felf in the Points that I have
' mentioned, I only add to what I have faid, That I do
' only own thefe things as my own Judgment, in thefe great
' and important Matters ; not willing that any thing wherein
' others may differ from me, fhould be looked upon as the
' Principles and Perfwafion of that Party whereto I adhere ;
' And I obteft, that no Man be fo Diabolick and Prophane,
' as to Charge this upon any of my Perfwafion, it being but
' my own ; in which I hope G O D hath approven me.
' And whom G O D Juftifeth, who dare Condemn ?

' Now, if the Lord, in his Wife and Over-ruling Provi-
' dence, bring me to the End of my Pilgrimage, and to my

' long

' long-looked for and defir'd Happinefs; let him take his
' own way and time in bringing me to it : And in the mean
' while, O my Soul, fing thou this Song, Spring up, O Well
' of this Happinefs and Salvation, of all this Eternal Hope
' and Confolation; and whilft thou art burthened with this
' Clog of a Clay Tabernacle, Dig thou Deep in it by Faith,
' Patience, Hope and Charity, and withal the Inftruments
' which G O D hath given thee; Dig in it both by Pre-
' cepts and Promifes; Dig carefully, and Dig continually,
' ay and till thou come to the Source and Head of the
' Fountain himfelf, from whence the Waters of Life flow
' forth; Dig until thou come to the Affembly of the Firft
' Born, when this Song is moft fuitably fung to the Praife
' and Glory of the rich Mercy and free Grace of this Foun-
' tain of Life : O my Soul, follow (in all this digging)
' the Direction of the great Law-giver; fo fhalt thou profper
' in all thy taking of Pains. O happy Nobles and Princes
' of *Ifrael*, who were admitted to the Sight and to the Song,
' to the Pains and to the Profit, which none of the mixed
' Multitude of Murmurers were admitted to becaufe of their
' unbelief, *Numb.* 21. 17. And O, Father of Mercy, while
' I am toffed upon the turbulent Seas of manifold troubles,
' grant that thy Prefence may be with me, and that thy
' Everlafting Arms may be underneath me to fupport me;
' for fure I am, *Mofes* thy Servant had good reafon to be
' importunate in this Suit, *Exod.* 32. 2. compared with 14
' and 15 *ver. Chap.* 34. 9. Seeing no lefs could furnifh him
' with frefh Supplies in the work he was about. O let thy
' Prefence be with me, and then my Soul fhall dig and fing,
' and fing and dig through times of trouble into Eternal
' Reft, where I fhall be admitted to behold the Rock
' Chrift, out of whom floweth the pure Fountain and River
' of Life and Happinefs, which I may drink and not be
' damnified through the Affaults of Satan, or the Invafions
' of Sin, or of a wicked World any more ; now according to
' thy Promife, *Matt.* 10. 19. Out of thy Fatherly Mercy
' grant prefent Help, Supply and Direction in this time of
' Trouble, feeing it is not in Man that walketh, to direct
' his own Steps, *Jer.* 10. 23. and tho' it be a hard thing
' rightly to diftinguifh betwixt Sin and Duty, yet thy Law,
' thy Word and thy Truth, which are quick and powerful,
' dividing afunder of Soul and Spirit, and is a Director of the
' Thoughts, and thy Law giveth Light, *Pfal.* 119. 105.
' *Pfal.* 32. 8. *For thy Teftimonies, O Lord, are fure, making*
' *wife the fimple, Pfal.* 19. 7. For thou alone canft make all thy
' Difpenfations prove profitable, in order to the purging away
' of

of Sin, even when they seem to be Destructive, Esa. 27. 9. Especially, when thou intends them not for Destruction, but for Tryal, Deut. 8. 2, 16. and for further Humiliaton; for thou, O Lord, hast led me for many Years through a barren and wearisom Wilderness, to the End that thou mayst work thy work of Mortification in me; altho', if it had seemed good unto thee, thou couldst have brought me into the Land of Promise and Rest a nearer way, Exod. 13. 17. For thou by Hardships, many a time hides Pride from Men, and sealest up their Instruction, that thou may'st deliver his Soul from the Pit, and that his Life may see the Light, Job. 33: 17. And although thou, O Lord, shouldst send me the back Tract and Tenor of my Life, to seek my Soul's Comforts and Incouragements from thence; yet I have no Cause to complain of hard, dealing from thy Hand, seeing it is thy ordinary way with some of thy People, Psal. 42. 6. O GOD, my Soul is cast down within me, therefore will I remember thee from the Land of Jordan and from the Hill Hermon, &c. Yea, the last time he brought me to the Banqueting-house, and made Love his Banner over me (amongst the Cold High-land Hills beside Kipper, November 1673.) he remembred his former Kindnesses towards me; but withal he spoke it in mine Ear, That there was a tempestuous Storm to meet me in the Face, which I behooved to go thro' with the strength of that Provision, 1 Kings 19. 7. And now, O my Soul, seeing it is his ordinary way and method with thee, to send a Shower and a Sunblink, and again a Sunblink and Shower; therefore, keep thou silent to GOD, and murmur not, fret not, be not disquieted, be still, and be content, seeing all my Persecutors can do, either by Fraud or Force, can neither alter the Nature or Kind of my Sufferings, or add so much as a Degree thereto, neither lengthen out the time of them for a Moment, Matth. 10. 29. Exod. 12. 41. All Pharaoh's Power could not keep Israel one Night longer in Ægypt; therefore it is my Duty to study with Paul, Phil. 4. 11, 12. Whatsoever state I am in, therewith to be content; and say, Shoud the Earth be forsaken, and the Rock be removed out of its Place for me? Job 18. 4. Should GOD alter the course of his Providence for me, in which there is such an Efficacy as to carry all things to the proper and appointed End: What an irresistable Power? And that I may be found in him, Not as having my own Righteousness which is of the Law, but that which is through the Faith of Christ, the Righteousness which is of God by Faith, Phil. 3. 9, 10, and to resign up unto GOD my Will

and

'and Affections, to be disposed as he pleaseth, and to say
'with Fear, Humility and Reverence, *O Father, not my Will,
'but thine be done*; and whether I live or dye, I may be
'the Lord's, that thro' his Mercy and Grace, I may attain
'to his Approbation, *viz. Well done, good and faithful Servant,*
'who hath hitherto sent his Angel, and *shut the Lyons Mouth
'that they have not hurt me*, Dan. 6. 22. And who hath so
'shut the Eyes of my Persecutors with a *Sodomitish* Blind-
'ness, that hitherto they could not find out the way how to
'break in upon me; and I hope he will in due time bring
'me out of the fiery Furnace, and shall not through his
'Grace suffer the smell thereof to be found upon me; and if
'not, yet I never held it to be my Duty, to worship this
'rotten and stinking Idol of Jealousie, which these Nations
'have set up, who have killed both the Lord Jesus and their
'own Prophets, and have Persecuted us, *Thes.* 1. 15. for
'*thou, O Lord, hast not abhorred nor despised my Afflictions
'when I was Afflicted, neither hast thou hid thy Face from me,
'but when I cryed unto thee thou heardest me,* Psal. 22. 24.
'*Now, O Lord God, thou hast made the Heaven and the Earth
'by thy great Power and stretched out Arm,* Jer. 37. 2. Bring
'thou me at length to a happy Arrival within the Gates of
'the *New Jerusalem,* where no unclean thing can come;
'that my Praise may be of Thee in the great Congregation.
'And altho' as *Job* saith, *Chap.* 10. 17. That thou, O
'Lord, hast deliver'd me to the ungodly; and hast turned
'me over into the Hands of the wicked, yet *by this I know,
'that thou, O Lord favourest me, because mine Enemies do not
'Triumph over me.* When I stand in Judgment, thou O
'Lord, didst not condemn; and if it pleaseth thee, they
'will not leave me in their Hands, *Psal.* 41. 11. *Psal.* 37. 33.
'But canst bring up my Life from the Pit of Corruption,
'*Jonah* 2. 6. And seeing I have not preferred, nor sought
'after mine own things, but thy Honour and Glory, the
'Good, Liberty and Safety of thy Church and People,
'altho' I may be now mis-constructed by many; yet at
'length I hope, thou, Lord, wilt make my Light break forth
'as the Morning, and my Righteousness as the Noon-day;
'and that Shame and Darkness shall cover all who are Ad-
'versaries to my Righteous Cause; for thou, Lord, art the
'Shield of my Help and the Sword of my Excellency, and
'my Enemies shall be found Lyars, *Amen,* yea and *Amen.*

JAMES MITCHEL.

In

IN some parts of this Villainous Paper, you find the Author Discoursing like a *Jesuit*, in some like an *Enthusiast*, and in many Places like *both*. And from the Beginning to the End of it, he Argues from the supposed Validity of the judicial Law, which GOD gave the *Israelites*, not as their GOD, but as their Political Sovereign; and which they on the other Hand received from his Infinite Majesty, not on a Moral Account, as his Rational Creatures, or the Sons of *Adam* or *Noah*; but upon the Account of the Civil Relation they had to him as Subjects, or his People in a Political Sense. For the *Jewish* Government, as all their Writers agree, was a *Theocratical* Constitution, or the Temporal Kingdom of GOD; who was pleased to become *Jehovah-Stater*, and dwell among them in a visible external Manner: In so much that the Judges and the Kings were but his High Commissioners and Vice-Roys, who were Chosen and Deposed by him at his Pleasure; and like *Moses* and *Joshua*, his first two Generals, could neither make War nor Peace, nor undertake any State-matter of great Moment, without first asking Council of the Lord.

Sometimes he Answered them by Messengers or Prophets, sometimes by Dreams and Visions, but most commonly in the time betwixt *Moses* and the Captivity, by *Urim* and *Thummim*, which was a Political Oracle, appointed on purpose for the Judges, Kings or Generals, or the whole Congregation to consult in Matters of State and War. But our Saviour, who came to Break down the Wall of Partition betwixt the *Gentiles* and the *Jews*, threw his Fathers Inclosure into the Common again, and put an End to his Political Government over the *Jews*. Who, had they embraced Christianity, and continued in their Country, as one entire People to this Day, would not have been obliged by their Specifick Judgments and Statutes, wherein their Civil, Criminal and Military Laws consist. No, the whole Design of the Gospel is so inconsistent with the *Jewish* Oeconomy, that it is impossible for Christians to observe some, ridiculous to observe others, and impious again to observe others of their judicial Laws. Of the last sort are all those which GOD gave the *Jews*; as *Carnifices Gentium*, or Executioners of his Wrath upon the seven Idolatrous incorrigble Nations, as likewise all those Capitals Acts against *Idolatry*, as High Treason to his Government, and inconsistent with the Design he had to be King, as well as GOD of the *Jews*, whom he set up as a Light among the *Gentiles*, and secured them by those great Severities from falling into

Damon-

Dæmonolatry, which was the Catholick Religion of the World.

This was the general Opinion of all Christians, till the Romanists began to argue by false Analogy from Things and Persons in the Jewish, to Things and Persons under the Christian Dispensation; and from them it was, that the Presbyterians first of all Learn'd to defend Murders, Affassi-nations, Rebellions and Massacres, as you see this Villain hath done.

Pope Adrian the Sixth, mov'd the Princes of Germany to cut off Luther and the Lutherans, because (forsooth) GOD cast Corah and his Company down into Hell, and Commanded, That all those should be put to Death that would not Obey the High Priest. And as Davila relates in the Ninth Book of his History, the Pope compared the Duke of Guise, that Patron of the Cursed League, to Judas Maccabæus, and the Jesuits complimented him with the name of Gideon, and bid him go on and prosper in the name of GOD. According to which damnable Notion of false Zealotry, when they Consecrate an Affassin (as Sospitian hath proved they some-times do) to Murder an Heretick Prince, they Solemnly Consecrate him to the Work of the Lord in such a like Form as this, Thou Blest Son of God, take here the Sword of Gideon, the Sword of Jeptha, the Sword of Sampson, the Sword of David, the Sword of the Maccabees, go, and be of good Courage, and the Lord strengthen thy Arm. Can any thing be more like Mr. Mitchel's Justification, than this? Would not one think his Soul had entred into that Secret of the Jesuits, seeing he hath not Acted only like one of their Affassins, but written his Apology with their poyson'd Ink. If Father Brown the Jesuit, that Preach'd among them so many Years, had Penn'd it, Could it have favour'd stronger of the Society of Jesu; or become such an Author better than it doth? He boasted on his Death-bed at Ingest-ombrigger, that he had Preach'd as down-right Popery in our Field-Conventicle, as ever he had Preach'd in Rome it self; and had he been the Author of this Paper, he might also have boasted, to the Comfort of his departing Soul, that he had written as true a Papistical Pamphlet, as ever was written in the Romish Church. I think there is great Presumption to Affert, That the Father might help to Indoctrinate Mitchel in this Mystery of Iniquity; but if he did not, yet both he and the Author of Naphthali might invent these Doctrines without consulting Jesuits, seeing it is the Cabala of their own Sect.

F

For

For this way of Arguing, to do Mischief from the judicial Law, was the Logick of our most Primitive *Presbyterians*, which hath ever since caused so much Ruin and Blood.

For in the Convention at *Edinburgh*, *January* 1560, for Ratification of a new Form of Church-Policy, it was Enacted, That all Monuments and Places of Idolatry, by name, Chapels, Cathedral-Churches and Colleges, should be suppress'd; whereupon through the Instigation of *John Knox* ensued (saith my *a* Author) a pitiful Vastation of Churches, and Church Buildings; so that the Libraries nor Church-Registers, nor Sepulchres of the Dead were spar'd. And some ill-advised Preachers (saith he) did Animate the People in their Barbarous proceedings, crying out, That Places, where *Idols* had been Worship'd, ought by the Law of G O D to be destroy'd; and that the sparing of them was the reserving of things Execrable; as if, (he subjoyns) the Commandment given to *Israel* for Destroying the Places where the *Canaanites* did Worship their false Gods, had been a Warrant for them to do the same. I confess, the *b* Council *of Carthage*, in the time of *Honorius*, Decreed, That the Emperors should be Petition'd to raze the Temples, and destroy the Reliques of Heathen Idols; but it was because in Maritime, and other Places of *Africk*, Idolatry was yet professed in them; and not from any Sense of Duty incumbent upon them from the *Mosaic* Law. For that, as well as the *Latin* and *Greek* Churches, had converted the Temples of *Idols* into the Churches of Christ; but as for the supernumerary, useless Company of them, which remain'd as Snares, and Monuments of the Dominion which the Devil had had in the World, they thought it both for the Honour and Interest of Christianity, that they should be taken away.

In the following Year, 1561, altho' Queen *Mary* had agreed with the Council, That she should have her own Service in her own Chapel, yet the next Day, when the *c* Tapers were carried through the Court, a Zealot of Mr. *Mitchel's* Principles fell upon him that bore them, and broke them all in Pieces; and had not the Tumult been timely suppress'd by some moderate Spirits, abominable Barbarities had ensued: For some maintain'd, That if Right were done, her Majesty's Priests should have been slain, according to GOD's Law against Idolaters. It would be endless to

---

a *Spotsw.* &c. in *Anno* 1560. L. 3.   b *Can.* 62.   c *Spotsw.* &c. L. 4. *Anno* 1561.

trace

trace thefe Principles down from the time of the Original Presbyterians to thefe unhappy Days; you may fee enough of them in the Parliament Sermons, and innumerable other Pamphlets of the late Times. How often did the late Presbyterian Preachers commend the Houfe of Commons for their Zeal, and ranfack the Old Teftament for Examples and Precepts to perfwade the giddy Vulgar, that the Rebels Fought the Lord's Battels, and that their Caufe was his? How often did they Compare the moft Active of them to *Gideon, Samfon* and *Phineas*, and Complement the Worthies of the late Long Parliament in *England*, as *Gregory* the 15th Complimented the laft King of *France*, when he raifed an Army for the Extirpation of the Proteftants, in the glorious Name of the Lord of Hofts. Did not that Darling of the Faction, Mr. *Calamy*, in the bloody Speech which he made in 43, at the *Guildhall* of *London*, to the Citizens, (to perfwade them to contribute largely towards the bringing in of our *Scottifh* Army) juftifie himfelf from the Objection of his own tender Confcience, that he being a Minifter of the Gofpel, fhould ftir them up to make War; by taking an Apology from *Numb.* 10. and *Deut.* 20. Where G O D ordain'd, that the Sons of *Aaron*, the Priefts, fhould found the Alarm with the Silver Trumpets; and that the Prieft fhould make a Speech to encourage the People going out to Battel, to Fight for the Lord of Hofts. So that *Naphthali, Nebufhtan*, and *Mitchel's* Papers, are but the laft Improvement of the Presbyterian Logick and Zeal; which makes our Conventicle-Preachers ride about with Guards, like petty Princes, and their Followers, more like Soldiers than Chriftians, come Armed by Thoufands into the Field.

They are now arriv'd at the higheft Pitch of Enthufiafm and Bigotry, and are as ready upon all Occafions, to do as much for the Spiritual Crown of Chrift, which they think inconfiftent with the Mitre; as the Men of the *Fifth Monarchy* Principles, are ready to do for the Temporal Kingdom of Jefus. So that if GOD in his good Providence had not fent down the Duke of *Lauderdale* among us, to prevent the Storm that was ready to arife; in all human Probability, this Kingdom had been involv'd in fuch a violent Rebellion, as could not have been quell'd without extrinfecal Force. His Grace came hither without any profpect of Trouble; and the incredible numbers of Nobility and Gentry, that throng'd to meet him feveral Days Journey on *Englifh* ground, were enough to make him prefume, that all would be quiet and ferene. But he had not been many Days among us, when he

wa

was surpriz'd with the News of great Insolencies and Disorders, caus'd by the Field-Conventicles in the West.

Now, to make you understand what Wind blew up that secret Flame, and how those evil Principles probably came to be put into Fermentation, I must lead you back to the Year 1674, when some, whose Discontents far exceeded their Causes, under the old Pretence of Redressing Grievances, did design something else, and thereby almost render'd the Parliament useless for the Publick Ends, for which it was call'd.

The Duke of Lauderdale was then His Majesty's High Commissioner; and there was not one real Grievance, of which he himself did not propose the Removal; nor any one pretended, concerning which he was not willing to Treat; And if it were found to be really such, to have it redress'd in an orderly, fair, and legal Manner, according to the Fundamental Constitutions of the House. But this would not satisfie their Discontents (which enough Demonstrates, that something else was design'd besides the Removal of Grievances) whereupon his Grace returning to Court to give an Account of Affairs to his Royal Master; such great Confusions appeared among us, as naturally follow palliated Discontents. Then did Welsh, and other declared Traytors, take the Confidence to Preach openly in Fife and Tweed-dale, which before had been orderly Places; and there they were entertain'd, and encourag'd to debauch the People from their Duty to the King, and the Church: And if these bold Attempts and disorderly Practices had not then been timely quell'd by his Grace's Care and Conduct, it is easie to Divine to what iminent Hazard, our Peace and Government had been expos'd.

Whether our Fanaticks were then under-hand encourag'd to commit these Insolencies by designing Male-contents, Time, the Revealer of Secrets, may shew; but it is beyond all Peradventure, that scandalous and unseasonable Divisions, caus'd by nothing but Envy and Discontent, did then Animate and Embolden them to these turbulent Practices; and therefore it seems not improbable, that the same Discontented Party, envying the Duke his glorious Reception, and the just Esteem he hath with his Prince, and intending to frustrate his best Councils and Endeavours for preserving this, and by Consequence the Kingdom of England in Peace, have now conjured up the Phanatick Spirit again, to Act in more insolent Irregularities, than at any time heretofore. But let the Cause be what it will, the Conventicles were never so numerous and frequent, as they now began, and

some;

sometime after continued to be in *Fife, Clidsdale, Tweat-dale, Galloway, Sterling-shire* and *Carrict*; the last of which Shires had always been Peaceable and orderly till now, when they all conspir'd to invade the publick Peace. At these Field-Conventicles, would meet sometimes five or six Thousand, sometime eight or nine Thousand at a time, as many of which as were fit to bear Arms, and could provide them, never fail'd to come appointed into the Field. For this Reason, our Laws and Proclamations stile these Field-Meetings, *Rendevouzes of Rebellion*, which is as modest a Name as they can deserve. For most of the Principal Preachers among them, as *Welsh* and *Arnott*, are either attainted or declared Traytors, and were Actors in the Rebellion of 66. and the *Harangues* (for I will not call them Sermons) which they make to the People, tend to nothing, but to make them Rebel, and possess them with Hatred against the King and the Church. In *October* last, at *Sanchil* in *Carrict*, Mr. *Welsh* attended with seven or eight seditious Preachers, made a Preachment to the principal Division of a Multitude upwards of 7000 People, upon St. *John* 11. 34, 35. In this Preachment among much other Treasonable Stuff, he spoke these Words, *The King, the Nobles and the Prelates, are sure the Murderers of Christ*; and then sitting down in his Chair, he said, *Oh People, I will be silent. Speak O People, and tell me what good the King hath done since his home-coming; yea, hath he not done all the Mischief a Tyrant could do?* At another Conventicle not long after, he spoke thus, or to this purpose, *That he was confident that GOD would yet assert the Cause of* Pentland-hills, *in spite of the Curates* (for so they call the Orthodox-Ministers) *and their Masters the Prelates; and in spite of the Prelates and their Master the King; and in spite of the King, and his Master the Devil.*

But to proceed, at these Field-Meetings, they Administred the Solemn League and Covenant to the People; and made them Swear never to hear the Orthodox Ministers more; and in a most Popish manner, gave them the Sacrament thereupon. They also kept Classical Meetings, where they Ordain'd Ignorant and Factious Striplings, and by an unparallell'd Act of Schism, took the Confidence to Re-ordain one Mr. *John Cuningham*, who was formerly Ordain'd Presbyter by the late Lord Bishop of *Galloway*; and likewise presum'd to receive the Hypocritical Confessions and Repentence of such as they had perswaded, or suborn'd to confess the great Sin of joining in Worship with our Church. They admitted Ruling Elders in several Precincts, and with

incom-

Incomparrble Impudence proceeded to Inftitute and Induct Preachers of their Tribe, both into vacant and full Churches; according to Mr. *Mitchel's* Judgment ; who afferts in his Apology, That every Parifh ought to choofe its Preacher, and that Patronage is but a Popifh Right. They alfo confiding in their Numbers, proceeded in manifeft Contempt of Authority to Erect Preaching-Houfes ; particularly in *Carrict* and *Galloway*, where Perfons of no mean Quality and Intereft, harbour'd and carefs'd thofe great Apoftles of the Caufe, *Welfh* and *Arnott* ; who ride about thefe dif-affected Shires in great State and Security, with Guards confifting of Forty, Fifty, or greater numbers of Horfe. From thefe Infolencies they proceeded to invade the Houfes, and menace the Perfons of fome Orthodox Minifters, whom Mr. *Welfh* declared either in a Conventicle, or *Presbytery*, fomewhere in *Carrict*, that it was as Lawful to Kill, as for the *Ifraelites* to Kill the *Canaanites*, if they complained to the Men (for fo he called the Magiftrates) in Power. Thefe Out-rages fo frighted the Orthodox-Clergy, that many Minifters forfook their Charges ; and fome of our Bifhops, who liv'd in thofe diftracted Corners, were forced for their Security to repair to this Town. Thus all Things feem'd to run into Confufion ; and if excellent Methods had not been ufed to prevent the Sequel of fuch dangerous Beginnings, the Faction by this Time had grown into a formed Party, and difputed *the Caufe* with an Army in the Field.

The firft Thing the Privy Council did, was to iffue out Proclamations for the Execution of the Laws againft thefe Conventicles, and to ufe all Means poffible for feizing the Perfons of *Welfh* and *Arnott*, and other feditious Preachers: But the former were render'd ineffectual, the Heritable Sheriff and Bayliffs, and other Officers of the feditious Diftricts refufing to Act ; and the latter could not be brought to Effect, becaufe the Preachers are always fo ftrongly guarded in Publick ; and in Private, fhelter themfelves with fuch fuperftitious Adorers of their holy Perfons, as none of the propofed Rewards can tempt to Betray. Diforders thus continuing, the Council acquainted His Majefty with the Dangers they Threatned ; and humbly mov'd him to fend fpeedy Orders, That a confiderable Number of his *Irifh* Troops fhould march to the Maritime Borders next adjacent to *Galloway*, and the Weftern Shires, to be ready for Tranfportation if Occafion requir'd. His Majefty, who was long fince acquainted with the Spirit and Principles of our *Remonftrator-Presbyterians*, in Compliance with the wholefome Advice of his Privy Council, immediately order'd, That a

well

well-appointed Party, of about 3000 Horse and Foot, should be sent under the Conduct of the Loyal and Valiant Viscount of *Granard*, our Country-man, to Quarter upon the Maritime Borders, and to March at the Command of the Privy Council here. This particular Care of his Majesty, and the Approach of the Forces, did very much surprize the Fanatical Party, who were made to believe by the Malecontents, that the Duke had no Interest at Court, nor was capable to procure any extrinsical Assistance, although they should Rebel. The *Irish* Forces being Arriv'd upon the Coasts, the Council were resolv'd to try what fair and gentle Means would do; and thereupon directed Letters to the Heritors (whom you call Landlords) of *Aire* and *Renfrew*, to know if they would undertake by their own Power to Reduce these Disorders, having the King's Authority for that Effect. The Heritors met in a full Assembly, and after two Days Consultation, return'd Answer by three Noble Lords, whom the Council had sent to attend them, That they could not undertake by their own Power to keep the Country free from Conventicles, or any Disorders that might ensue thereupon.

You must know that our Landlords have far more Authority over their Tenants, than yours; insomuch, that in the most disaffected Places, there are no Conventicles where the Heritors and Superiors use their private Authority to keep the People constant to the Church. All the World here knows, that there is not a more Fanatical Shire in this Kingdom than *Murray*; and yet by the single Authority and Interest of that most Loyal and Deserving Person the Earl of *Murray*, it is kept in as perfect Order and Obedience, as if there were no Conventicles in the World. But, as for the aforesaid Shires, the Council expected no such Answer from them, because they of all others have had most Indulgence, as having Non-conforming Ministers legally setled in very many Churches among them; which one would think, if that Party had any Reason, Modesty or Conscience, might have kept them from troubling the publick Peace. Therefore the Council having receiv'd such an unreasonable Answer from the Heritors of these more indulged Shires, concluded what Returns they might expect from others; and therefore began now to think it was high time to reduce them to their Duty by Force. Whereupon, knowing that the Body of this Kingdom was Loyal, they resolv'd rather to reduce the Fanaticks by our own intrinsical Power, than to call in his Majesties *Irish* Forces, unless there should be absolute Need. Wherefore, to the

King's

King's ſtanding Forces, they added the *Militia* of the moſt Loyal County of *Angus*, and admitted the *Auxiliary* Forces which ſeveral Loyal Lords that have Intereſt and Authority in the *Highlands*, did proffer to raiſe out of their Vaſſals and Dependents for his Majeſties ſpecial Service in this critical Exigence of Affairs, And by his Majeſties ſpecial Approbation and Command, they were all United into one Army, under the Conduct of the moſt Valiant and Loyal Earl of *Lin Lithgow*, who towards the latter End of laſt *January* march'd into the Weſtern Shires.

And that all things might be tranſacted in a fair, legal and orderly Manner, there is alſo ſent along with the Army a Committee of the Privy Council, conſiſting of Eleven Right Honourable Perſons, who are inveſted with ſufficient Power, Civil and Criminal, to puniſh all ſorts of Offenders, and are now ſteadily purſuing thoſe great Ends for which they were ſent thither. There's a ſtrict Correſpondence betwixt them and the Privy Council, to whom they ſend frequent Accounts of their Proceedings; and from whom they receive ſuch Meaſures and Directions, as may moſt conduce to reduce and ſecure thoſe diſorderly Shires. To which purpoſe, in the firſt Place, they proceed to diſarm them, cauſing all ſuſpected Perſons to deliver their Arms (whereof great Proviſion was made) to their reſpective Sheriffs upon Oath, who are to deliver them to the Major General, and to be ſent by him to his Majeſties Garriſons. They have likewiſe Order to plant Garriſons in what Places ſoever they ſhall think fit, and have proceeded to do Execution on the new Built Meeting-houſes, thoſe Temples of *Baal Berith*, by Commanding that they ſhould be pull'd down, and that their Materials ſhould be Burnt. They are likewiſe to tender a *Bond* to be taken by all Heritors; wherein, as Maſters of Families, they are to be Bound for themſelves, their Wives, Children and Servants; and, as Landlords, for their Tenants and Cottagers, That they ſhall not go to Conventicles, nor Receive or Supply Conventicle-Miniſters, but live orderly in Obedience to the Law; ſo that if their Wives, or any of their Children or Servants Tranſgreſs, they will be bound to undergo the legal Penalties for them. But in caſe their Tenants or Cottagers Tranſgreſs, they will be Bound to Preſent them to Juſtice, or turn them off their Tenements, or elſe to be liable to the Penalties they ſhall incur.

The

The Form of this Bond, or Civil Anti-
covenant, was drawn up by the Privy
Council, and is as followeth :

I A. B. *under subscribing, do faithfully bind
and oblige me, That I, my Wife, Bairns, and Servants
respectively, shall be no ways present at any Conventicles, and
disorderly Meetings in time coming ; but shall live orderly in
Obedience to the Law, under the Penalties contained in the
Acts of Parliament made there anent. As also, I bind and
oblige me, that my whole Tenants and Cotters respectively, their
Wives, Bairns and Servants shall likewise refrain, and abstain
from the said Conventicles, and other illegal Meetings not
Authorized by the Law, and that they shall live orderly in Obedience to the Law. And further, that I, nor they shall Recept,
Supply or Commune with forfeited Persons, intercommuned
Ministers, or vagrant Preachers, but shall do our utmost endeavour to apprehend their Persons. And in case my said Tenants,
Cotters, and their fore-saids shall Contravene ; I shall Take or
Apprehend any Person, or Persons guilty thereof, and present
them to the Judge Ordinar, that they may be Fined or Imprison'd
therefore, as is provided in the Acts of Parliament made there
anent. Otherwise I shall remove them and their Families from
off my Ground. And if I shall fail herein, I shall be liable to
such Penalties as the said Delinquents have incurred by the
Laws, consenting to the Registration hereof in the Books of
his Majesty's Privy Council, or Books of any other Judges com-
petent, that Letters and Executorials may be direct hereupon
in Form as Effeirs and Constitutes my Procurators.*

This is the Tenor of the Bond ; and lest the Force thereof
should be eluded, the Privy Council have declar'd, That
every Heritor, that shall receive into his Lands or Service,
any Tenants or Servants of any other Heritor, without a
Certificate from him, or the Minister of the Parish where
they liv'd, that they liv'd orderly as to this Matter, shall
be subject to such Fines as the Privy Council shall think fit
to inflict, to punish them for their Crime, and repair the
Damage that shall accrue to the Heritor or Master, whose
Tenants or Servants they did receive. All the Lords of the
Privy Council and the Judges (whom we call the Senators
of the College of Justice) together with the Advocates

G   Writers,

Writers, and all others belonging to the Society of the Lawyers, have taken this Bond, as also the Lords of the Exchequer and the Justiciary Lords, which is a very prevalent. Example; and little doubt is made, but the Generality of the Subjects of the Nation will chearfully Sign it, as being so beneficial to Authority, and so proper an Expedient to recover the common People into their Wits. And it cannot possibly give the least umbrage of Scruple to the Conscience of the most weak and peevish Dissenter; being nothing but a purely civil alternative Obligation, to do what the Law requires, or submit to the Penalties therein contain'd. Perhaps it may seem strange in *England*, that a Landlord should be Bound in this manner for his Tenants; but there is nothing more reasonable and customary here, because our Heritors have such a despotic Power over their Tenants, as you cannot well imagine, unless you had liv'd here.

And in case any Persons shall finally refuse to take this Bond (as some *Fife* and *Western* Gentlemen have made difficulty at it) the Privy Council (according to the legal and uncontroverted Practice of that Board in all Ages) hath Ordain'd, that Letters shall be directed to them, to charge them forthwith to give in Security to his Majesty's Privy Council, that They, their Wives, Children, Tenants and Servants, shall keep his Majesty's Peace, and particularly that they shall not go to Conventicles, nor harbor Rebels nor intercommuned Persons; and that they shall keep the Persons, Families, and Goods of their regular Ministers harmless, under the double of every Man's valued Yearly Rent, if he have any, or of such Penalties as shall be thought Convenient by his Majesty's Council or their Committee, if they have none; which if they shall refuse to do within six Days next after the Charge, they are to be declared his Majesty's Rebels (as the manner is here) with Sound of an Horn.

To conclude, the Committee is to proceed to the condign Censuring of such, as shall appear upon Proof to have harboured *Welsh* or *Arnott*, or other intercommuned Persons, and such also as have Invited or Convocated the silly People unto the Field-Assemblies, under pretence of hearing Sermons, and such as contributed by Money, Work, or Materials to build the new *Samaritan*-Synagogues; two of which the Earl of *Cassels* was commanded to Demolish in *Carrick*, as was his Duty to have done before.

All this hath been done under the wise Conduct of the Duke of *Lauderdale*, to whose presence among us, next
under

under GOD, this poor Church and Religion are redeemable, that they have been preserved from Confusion and Blood. And I question not, but his vigorous Endeavours to suppress this Schism (the like whereof in all respects, was never yet heard of in any Age or Nation) have by this time, effectually confuted all the lying Reports that were sent into *England* by our Men of Schism and Faction, with a Design to render him odious in our Neighbour Countrey, and discredit his Administration here.

But I beg Mr. *Mitchel's*, and your Pardon, for leaving him so long. I could not forbear to interfert this Account of his Western Brethren, whose Confessor he liv'd, and whose Martyr he dy'd. I'll now return to visit him again, and leave him no more till I see him in his Grave.

In the Interval betwixt his Condemnation and Execution, he seldom spoke of his approaching **Death**, but as of a Martyrdom or Murther; and glory'd that he was accounted worthy to suffer for Christ. This is the Stile of his short Speech, and the frequent Visits, Papers and Messages that he receiv'd from the Brotherhood, to Dye with Courage in the *Cause*; and to Seal the Truth, that is, the *Covenant*, with his Blood; together with the frequent Debauches which he made with Ale, Wine and Brandy, contributed very much to heighten his Obstination, and make him insensible of his Crime.

You cannot imagine, how much the Fanaticks of all Parts were concern'd about him. From the West, a private Message was sent to the Archbishop, to assure his Grace, That if Mr. *James Mitchel* were Hang'd, another should not fail to Execute his Design. His Majesty's Advocate, who pursu'd him, receiv'd a threatning anonymous Letter; and the common Talk of this Town was, That Mr. *James Mitchel's* Blood should be Reveng'd upon the whole Order: And truly, I doubt not, but if all the Fathers of our Church, and all the Clergy under them, had but one Neck, that there are at least 500 Covenanted *Mitchel's* behind, that would strive to cut it off.

In the Year 1668, when he made the Attempt, the Fanatical Party made a Sport of it; and, as if the Ruin of the Church were to follow upon it, many fair Pretenders, that out of Compliance to Authority, had hitherto given our Bishops that particular Veneration, that was due to their Character, began now to slight them, and would scarce give them that common Respect which was due to other Men. The like Charge was observ'd upon the late Insolencies of the *Whigs* in th: *West*; the Respect of our Bishops and

and Episcopal Clergy, began visibly to decay, and some that were then in a Condition to do the Faction a kindness, had the Confidence to say, That they knew no Reason there was to oppose the Inclinations of the People, to support about a dozen Men.

And while this Martyr of Iniquity lay in Goal, the Mouths of our Fanaticks were full of Railing against the Bishops ; and the Rascality, who are often taught to speak the sence of greater Persons, were hear'd to say, That it were better the Primate should be Hang'd than he. In the *Octave* betwixt his Sentence and Execution, he receiv'd, as I was credibly inform'd, 400 Dollars in private Gifts, which was interpreted by the Party for the particular Care that GOD had of him, who never sees *the Righteous forsaken, nor his Seed begging their Bread.*

The Day before his Execution, he sent to the Provost, or Mayor of *Edinburgh*, to desire a Stage larger than ordinary, because he had a great number of Friends, that intended to appear at his Execution in Mourning ; but his Lordship was more honest and prudent, than to grant the vain-glorious Villain his desire. When he was upon the Ladder, he called a *Psalm* to be sung. When the *Psalm* was ended, he took out of his *Psalm*-book two Copies of his intended *Speech*, which he threw among the People ; for there had he put them to elude the search. After his Body was cut down, it was conveigh'd to *Magdalen*-Chapel ; from whence it was carried to Burial in great Pomp, being attended with at least 40 Mourners, whereof the *Justice General's Gentleman* was one. 'Tis reported also, that the Hearse-Cloth was of Velvet, but certain it is, it was more than ordinary brave.

The Evening before his Execution, Information was brought to the Provost, That the Women of *Edinburgh* (I mean the Fanatical Part of them) had enter'd into a Conspiracy to rescue him between the Prison and the Gallows ; which obliged his Lordship to provide extraordinary Guards, capable to prevent any such Design. This Information was well grounded, if it were not true ; for there was never seen such an Appearance of that Sex at any Execution, as was at his, where a Body of at least seven Hundred Sisters stood together almost in *Rank* and *File.*

The next Morning after his Execution, there were several Copies of his Speech distributed, and Verses put up in several Places of the City,

The

The following Satyr in *Scottish* I got a Copy of, which I here present unto you, Entitled as it was, to the Memory of Mr. *James Mitchel.*

O-Y-ES O-y-es Covenanters,
   Filthy, Cruel, lying Ranters;
Come here, and see your murdering Martyr
Sent to Hell i'th' Hangman's Garter;
Your Sealing Witnesses we bear
Are Mr. James Mitchel and Major Weir:
One with his Hand, but had na Pith;
Th'other your Wives know well wherewith;
Which makes them sigh, and sighing say,
Welsh can but Preach, but Weir could Pray.
It's this that all Religion shames,
To give Hell's Vices Heavenly names.
Then Devils, then cast off your Masks;
Murder and Whoredom are your Tasks,
Which you to all the World proclaim,
Boasting and Glorying in your Shame;
And say your Covenant doth allow
This, Maugre your Baptismal Vow;
And that the holy Oath doth bind you
To leave such holy Seed behind you.
For at, and after your long Prayers,
You lye together Pairs by Pairs;
And every private Meeting Place
Is made a Bawdy-house of Grace:
You shew it is your loving Natures,
To be sweet fellow-feeling Creatures.
But to profane your Holy Order
With Incest, Buggery and Murder,
Is plainly to proclaim you Devils,
And horrid Crimes to be no Evils.
Mr. James Mitchel lay four Year
In Grissald's House with Major Weir;
And from his Ghostly Father learns
To lye with Women and get no Bairns,
The Mystery of the Tribe, a Trick
Makes all the Women mad Fanatick:
And now they both in Hell are met,
Where for your Company they wait.

Then

Then fill your Measure, and post on
To your deserv'd Damnation.
Go Whore and Bugger, Kill and Pray,
Till every Dog shall have his Day;
Or go together to Hell in Troops,
Else strive for new Grass-market Loops.
He that Whores best, and Murders most,
Of him the Sect shall always boast;
And put him, as they've put Mas James,
Among their Saints and Martyrs Names.

YOU see the *West* is a Place above all others of this Kingdom, wherein Fanaticism most abounds. This must needs awaken your Curiosity to enquire from what Magnetism it is, that our Conventicle-preachers have acquir'd such a strong Verticity to that Point. Truly, the Reason is the same for which yours haunt *London*, and the most opulent Towns and Counties of *England*, even the Riches of the Place. There's a necessity laid upon them to Preach the Gospel there; yea, wo unto them if they Preach it not in *Fife* and the *West*, where so many Rich Traders, and Heritors live. But as for the *Highlands*, and other poorer Counties, they have no Christian Compassion for them, but let them live and dye in Ignorance and Idolatry; because their Souls are not so precious for want of Silver and Gold. I remember when I was at *London* in 76. I heard a Famous Conventicle Minister say, That if it were not for the Non-conforming Ministers, Thousands of Souls in that populous City, would starve for want of the Word. I very much wonder'd to hear him say so, considering how many Hundred Sermons were Preached every Week by the Orthodox Ministers, and the best, I thought, that ever I had heard. But being the next Day in some Company, which was discoursing about the Conventicles, one or two of them began to tell of the great store of Money the Conventicle-Preachers had in the Banks, and how some of them kept their Coaches, and he believ'd it would not be long e're their Wives kept their Chairs. Then I began to understand the Reason of the great Care those Gentlemen had to feed the Souls of the good Citizens; and was very glad, that to keep a Coach was no longer a sign of *Prelatical* Pride. When I return'd home, I told our *Whig*, that the Non-conformists Ministers of *London* began to keep Coaches; but the greatest part of them would not believe me; and those that did, said with sighs, they were sorry, that there

were

were *Diotrephefes* among them, that lov'd the Pre-eminence; and that GOD would have a Controverfie with them for their *Prelatical Pride.* The like I have feen in a Preface to a *Presbyterian* Treatife of Divinity, Printed about that Time, wherein the Author complains of the *Prelatical Spirit,* that began to fhew it felf among the Non-conforming Minifters; whereof fome living in great Plenty and State, contemned others who were Poor, and whofe Lot was fallen in Places, where Perfecution did abound.

In the *Scottifh* Verfes, you fee the Poet upbraids their Baptifmal Vow with the Covenant; not, as I conceive, upon the common Account, as another Poet may do, but becaufe 'tis the frequent Practice of our *Whig-Preachers* to Baptize the Children of their Difciples into the *Solemn League and Covenant,* as well as into the *Covenant of Grace.* He alfo takes Notice of the intimate Familiarity betwixt Mr. *Mitchel* and Major *Weir*; and unlefs you will be at the Pains to read the Life of the latter, as well as the former, you'll never be able to underftand the Satyr, nor know whether the Satyrift's Indignation be juft or unjuft. I'll promife you the Narrative fhall affect you both with Wonder and Indignation; tho' for the Honour of our Nature and Religion, I wifh no fuch Stories were extant in the World. Nay, confident I am, that when you have confider'd it in all the Circumftances that attend it, you will fay, that he was one of the moft prodigious Sinners that ever was extant of human Race : For there's nothing in Hiftory comparable to him, nor I hope will ever be ; and had not our Bleffed Saviour told us, that Men may be fo wicked, as to Sin be-yond Forgivenefs, I could fcarce have believ'd that any Man, much lefs a Chriftian, could have committed *Un-cleannefs* in all Species, with Women, Devils and Beafts.

But fuch a Monfter was this *Pharifee,* of whom I am going to give you an Account; which is taken out of the public Regifter of our Criminal Court, and the Authority of Perfons of known Integrity, and great Reputation in the World.

Thomas Weir was Born and Bred in the Weftern Parts of this Kingdom; where he was early prepoffeffed with the Principles of Schifm and Rebellion, which he fhew'd upon all occafions, particularly in the Beginning of the late Re-bellion, wherein he was a forward Stickler, and by his ex-traordinary Zeal for the *Caufe,* raifed himfelf to a greater Command in fome Troop or Company, than Men of his mean Original ufe to arrive unto here. About the Year 1649, he had the great Truft of the Guards of this City committed unto him under the Quality of *Major*; and from that time to the Day of his infamous Death, was always called by the Name of Major *Weir*. He behav'd himself in this Office with great Cruelty and Insolence towards the Loyal Party, being very active in discovering and apprehending the Cavaliers, and bringing them to be Arraign'd and Try'd for their Lives. He used to Insult and Triumph over them in their Miseries, and Persecute them with all manner of Sarcasms and Reproaches, when they were led out like Victims to publick Execution; as many yet alive can testifie to the World. In particular, this barbarous Villain treated the Heroick Marquess of *Montross*, with all imaginable Insolence and Inhumanity when he lay in Prison; making his very Calamities an Argument, that GOD, as well as Man, had forsaken him; and calling him *Dog*, *Atheist*, *Traytor*, *Apostate*, *Excommunicate Wretch*, and many more such intollerable Names. This cruel Manner after which he used to outrage the poor Royalists, pass'd among the People for extraordinary Zeal; and made them consider him as a singular Worthy, whom GOD had raised up to support the *Cause*. He studied the Art of Dissimulation and Hypocrisie, always affecting a formal Gravity and Demureness in his Looks and Deportment; and employing a vast and tenacious Memory, which GOD had given him, in getting without Book, such Words and Phrases of the Holy Scriptures, as might serve best in all Companies to make him pass for an Holy and Gifted Man. He had acquir'd a particular Gracefulness in Whining and Sighing, above any of the sacred Clan; and had learn'd to deliver himself upon all serious Occasions, in a far more ravishing Accent, than any of their Ministers could attain unto. By these, and other Hypocritical Arts, he had got such a Name for Sanctity and Devotion, that happy was the Man with whom he would converse, and blessed was the Family in which he would vouchsafe to Pray.

For he pretended to Pray only in the Families of such as were Saints of the highest Form; insomuch, that the Brethren and Sisters of these Precincts, would strive who should have him to Exercise in their Houses; and of those that liv'd at a greater distance, some would come forty or fifty Miles to have the Happiness to hear him Pray. He had indeed, but by what Assistance will be seen hereafter, a wonderful fluency in extemporary Prayer, and what thro' Enthusiastical Phrases, Extasies and Raptures, into which he would appear Transported, he made the amazed People presume he was actuated by the Spirit of GOD. Besides

praying

praying, he us'd to Exhort and Bless the Families in which he Pray'd; but he never undertook to Preach in them, for fear of invading the Ministerial Province, which certainly would have offended the *Kirk*.

After this Manner, and in this mighty Reputation he liv'd 'till the Year 1670, which was the 70th Year of his Age: When, like the Tyrant *Tiberius*, after so many Murthers, and forts of unnatural Lusts, he was no longer able to endure the Remorse of his awakened Conscience, but to ease the Inquietudes of his guilty Mind, was forced to accuse himself, which he first of all did among those of his own Party, and desir'd them to bring him to publick Justice to expiate for his abominable Crimes. But they, confidering what a confounding Scandal and Dishonour, the Hypocrifie of fuch an eminent Profeffor would reflect upon the whole Sect, did with all poffible Care and Induftry, ftrive to conceal the *Major's* Condition, which they did for feveral Months, till one of their own Minifters, whom they efteem'd more forward than wife, Reveal'd the Secret to the Lord *Abbotshall*, then Provoft of *Edinburgh*; who judging human Nature uncapable of fuch horrid Crimes, as the Minifter told him the *Major* had confeffed, concluded he was fallen into a Phrenzy, or high degree of Melancholy; and therefore courteoufly fent fome Phyficians of his own Perfwafion and Acquaintance, to vifit him, and Phyfick him for his diftemper'd Brain. But the Phyficians, returning to the Provoft, affur'd him, That the *Major* was in good Health, and that he was free of Hypocondriack Diftempers, and had as found Intellectuals as ever; and that they believ'd his Diftemper was only an exulcerated Confcience, which could not be eas'd, till he was brought to condign Punifhment, as with Cryings and Roarings, he defir'd to be. Afterwards the Provoft, for his further fatisfaction, fent fome Conventicle-Minifters to enquire into his Condition, and make a report thereof; who finding it impoffible to difguife the Matter, which now was Town-talk, told his Lordfhip, That the *Major* was not affected with Melancholy, but that the Terrors of G O D, which were upon his Soul, urg'd him to Confefs, and Accufe himfelf. The Provoft therefore began to conclude, that he had good grounds to take publick Notice of this Affair; and therefore without further Enquiry, fent the Guards of the City to feize upon the *Major* and his Sifter, who was involv'd in his Confeffions, and carry them both to the publick Goal. There they were vifited by Perfons of all Sorts and Qualities, Clergy-men, Lay-men, Phyficians,

Lawye.s,

Lawyers, Conforming and Non-conforming Ministers, who all flock'd thither to see this Monster, and Discourse with him about his horrible Crimes.

They had not been long in Prison, before they were brought to Tryal, which was on the Ninth of *April*, 1670. They were Try'd before that Learned Civilian, Mr. *William Murray* and Mr. *John Prestoune*, Advocates, who were made Judges by Commission for that Time. They were Pursued by his Majesty's last Advocate, Sir *John Nisbett*, and the Jury by which they were Try'd, was *Gideon Shaw* Stationer; *James Penderer*, Vintner; *James Thompson*, Felt-maker; *Robert Brown*, Stationer; *James Brown*, Felt-maker; *Robert Johnstan*, Skinner; *John Cleghorn*, Merchant; with many more sufficient Citizens of *Edinburgh*, most of which, together with the greatest part of the Witnesses hereafter mention'd, are yet alive.

The Court being set, the *Major's* Indictment was read, the Sum of which was contain'd in these Four Particulars; *First, That he Enticed and Attempted to Defile his German Sister,* Jane Wear, *when she was but ten Years Old, or there-about; and that he lay with her when she was sixteen Years Old, while they both dwelt with their Father; and afterwards had frequent carnal Dealing with her in the House of Wicket-Shaw, in her younger Years: And lastly, That after she was forty Years Old, he lived in a State of Incest with her, in his House at Edinburgh, where they dwelt together many Years.*

Secondly, *That he committed Incest with* Margaret Bourdon, *Daughter to* Mein, *his Deceased Wife.*

Thirdly, *That he committed frequent Adulteries during the Life of his said Wife, both with Married and Unmarried Women; and particularly with* Bessy Weems, *his Servant-Maid, whom he kept in his House for the space of twenty Years, during which time, he lay with her as familiarly as if she had been his Wife.*

Fourthly, *That to his Fornications, Adulteries and Incests, he proceeded to add the Unnatural Sin of Beastiality, in lying with* Mares *and* Cows; *particularly in Polluting himself with a Mare upon which he rode, into the West Country, near* New-Mills. *All which Crimes particulariz'd in manner aforesaid, he acknowledged judicially at the Bar.*

The Sum of his Sister's Indictment, is reducible to these two Heads, First, *To the Charge of Incest, which she committed with her Brother: And Secondly, To the Charge of Sorcery and Witchcraft, but most especially of consulting Witches, Necromancers and Devils; and yet more particularly for keeping and conversing with a Familiar Spirit, while she liv'd at* Dalkeith,

keith, which us'd to Spin extraordinary quantities of Yarn Job-ber, in a shorter time than three or four Women could have done the same. All which she judicially confessed in the Face of the Court.

Then they proceeded to Swear the Witnesses, which the Lord Advocate call'd for further Probation against them both. Of these, *John Oliphant*, *William Johnston* and *Archibald Hamilton*, Aldermen of *Edinburgh* Depon'd, That on the *Monday* preceeding the *Major's* Arraignment, he did freely confess and declare unto them, That he had committed frequent Incest with his Sister *Jane*; divers Fornications and Adulteries with other Persons; and Beastiality with a *Mare* and a *Cow*. Master *John Sinclair*, a Conventicle-Minister, Depon'd, That the Day before his Tryal, he freely confessed unto him, that he was guilty of Adultery, Incest and Beastiality; and that his Sister had been often taken out of Bed from him: Whereupon asking him if he had ever seen the Devil, he answer'd, That he had felt him in the Dark. But as to his Conversation with the Devil, the Deponent might have declared more; for he had confessed to him and many others, particularly to the Lord Bishop of *Galloway*, then Minister of *Edinburgh*, that he had lain with the Devil in the shape of a Beautiful Woman.

Margaret Weir, Wife to *Alexander Weir*, Bookseller in *Edinburgh*, Testify'd, That when she was of the Age of 17 Years, or thereabouts, she found the *Major* her Brother, and her Sister *Jane*, lying together in the Barn at *Wicket-Shaw*; and that they were both Naked in the Bed together, and that she was above him, and that the Bed did Shake, and that she heard some scandalous Language between them in particular, that her Sister said, she was confident she should prove with Child. Furthermore, she Deponed, That *Catharine Cooper*, a Servant of the *Major's*, told her, That he had lain with *Margaret Bourdon* his Wife's Daughter; so that she would stay no longer in the House.

Anne, Wife to *James Simpson*, Bookbinder in *Edinburgh*, declared, That on *Monday* preceeding, and that Day in the Morning, that he confessed to her he had committed Incest with his Sister *Jane*, and *Margaret Bourdon* his Wife's Daughter; as likewise Beastiality with a *Mare* in the West-Country; and that he had Carnally conversed with his Maid-servant *Bessy Weems* for two and twenty Years.

Mr. *Archibald Nisbett*, Writer to the Signet, Declared, That in the Year 51 or 52, it was reported in the Country, that the *Major* had committed Beastiality with a *Mare* next

New-

Mills; and that he heard it reported the fame Day, in which it was faid he did the Fact. Mr. *John Alexander* of *Leith*, Deponed the fame, and faid he was then but half a Mile from the Place. After thefe Depofitions, the *Major* being Examin'd about his Act of Beaftiality, declared, That a Gentleman having given him a Mare, he rode upon her into the Weft-Country to fee fome Friends, and dealt Carnally with her near *New-Mills*; and that a Woman faw him in the Act, and complained of him to Mr. *John Nave* the Minifter of *New-Mills*; at whofe inftance he was brought back to the Place by fome Soldiers, but was there difmiffed for want of further Probation. And further being asked about the time, he anfwer'd, That to the beft of his Remembrance, it was when the Lords, Gentlemen, and Heritors were taken by the *Englifh* at *Elliot*.

As for Probation againft *Jane Weir*, the Lord Advocate infifted on her own Declaration, and all the Depofitions, in which as a Party fhe was involv'd. And being asked if fhe knew any thing concerning the Correfpondence that was faid to be betwixt the Devil and her Brother; fhe declared, that fhe had a long time been jealous of it, but was not certain; and that fix or feven Years before, fhe had found a Mark upon his Shoulder, like that which is called the Devil's Mark, at which fhe was fore afraid.

The Procefs being thus Ended, the Jury did unanimoufly find the *Major* Guilty of Inceft with his Sifter, and Beaftiality with a Mare and with a Cow, and found him Guilty of Adultery and Fornication by a Plurality of Votes. They alfo unanimoufly brought in *Jane* Guilty of Inceft with her Brother; whereupon the Deputed Judges Sentenced him to be Strangl'd at a Stake betwixt *Edinburgh* and *Leith*, on *Monday* following the 11th of *April*, and his Body to be Burnt to Afhes; and Condemned her to be Hang'd on the *Tuefday* following, in the *Grafs-Market* of *Edinburgh*.

Thus far have I given you a *juridical* Account of the deteftable Crimes of this Hypocritical Monftrous Man; I now proceed to acquaint you with fome other particulars, no lefs furprizing than the former; which upon ftrict enquiry I have Reafon to believe to be as true, as thofe that are judicially prov'd.

When they were feiz'd, fhe defir'd the Guards to keep him from laying hold on a certain Staff, which, fhe faid, if he chanc'd to get into his Hand, he would certainly drive them all out of Doors, notwithftanding all the Refiftance they could make. This Magical-Staff was all of one piece, with a crooked Head of Thorn-wood: She

said

said he receiv'd it of the Devil, and did many wonderful
things with it; particularly that he used to lean upon it in
his Hypocritical Prayers; and after they were Committed,
she still desir'd it might be kept from him; because if he
were once Master of it again, he would certainly grow Ob-
durate, and retract the Confessions which he had so publickly
made. *Apollonius Thyaneus* had such a Magical Staff as
this, which I believe was a Sacramental Symbol which the
Devil gave to the *Major*, and the Court had some such
Apprehensions of it, for it was order'd by the Judges to be
Burnt with his Body.

  She also confessed in Prison, That she and her Brother had
made a Compact with the Devil; and that on the 7th of
September, 1648, they were both Transported from *Edinburgh* to *Musselborough*, and back again, in a Coach and six
Horses, which seemed all on Fire, and that the Devil then
told the *Major* of the defeat of our Army at *Preston* in
England; which he confidently reported in most of its Cir-
cumstances several Days before the News had Arrived here.
This Prediction did much increase the high Opinion the
People began to have of him, and served him to make
them believe, that, like *Moses*, he had been with G O D
in the *Mount*, and had a Spirit of Prophesie as well as of
Prayer. But as for her Self, she said, She never receiv'd
any other Benefit by her Commerce with the Devil, than
a constant supply of an extraordinary quantity of Yarn,
which she was sure (she said) to find ready for her upon the
Spindle, whatever Business she had been about.

  Besides the Bestialities which the *Major* judicially acknow-
ledged he had Committed with the Mare and Cow, he
confessed he had done the same Abominations with three
Species more; and the Woman that delated him for the
Fact near *New-Mills*, was by order of the Magistrates of
Lanerk, Whipp'd through the Town by the Hand of the
Common Hang-man, as a Slanderer of such an eminent
holy Man.

  The Fornications and Adulteries which this ἀλογευόμενον
(as Buggerers are † call'd by the Council of *Ancyra*) Committed with the most Sanctimonius and Zealous Women of
the Sect, are too numerous to be related here. He had got
himself the Privilege, under a pretence of Praying and
Exhortation, to go to their Houses, and into their Bed-
Chambers when he pleas'd; and it was his Practice to visit
Married Women at such times especially as their Husbands
were

† *Can.* 16.

were from Home : : One especially, who liv'd in the Street called the West-bow in Edinburgh ; he had several times sollicited in her Husband's Absence to gratifie his unclean Desires ; till at last, wearied out with his Importunity, she told him how she abhorr'd his Design, and charg'd him never to come more to her House. Upon this he forbore to visit her for some time, till one Night, when she was undress'd and ready to step into Bed, the Major suddenly appears standing by her, at which she was so extreamly frighted, that she fell into a Swoun ; she had no sooner recover'd, but the Major endeavour'd to comfort and assure her, and confirm her against that strange surprize ; and renewing his Addresses, he Tempted her with many Arguments and filthy Speeches, and Gesticulations, telling her he had taken that Marvellous way of appearing in Private with her, on purpose to secure her Reputation ; that he would go out of her House in a manner as invisible as he came in. But she by this time having recover'd her usual Courage and Strength, push'd him off with violence, and cry'd out for help to her Maid ; upon which he immediately disappear'd. The Windows and Doors were all close shut, and I make little doubt, but his Coachman to the fiery Coach, conveigh'd him in and out through the Chimney, or perhaps by the Door, which the cursed Familiar might open and shut again, as well as the Angel of the Lord did unlock and lock the Prison-Door, wherein the Apostles were put.

As for the miserable Woman, she was never well after this Magical manner of Address, which the lusty Satyr made unto her ; but immediately fell into a deep Melancholy, which ended in a languishing Sickness, whereof not many Weeks after she Died. And when she was upon her Death-bed, she declared this strange Story to many Persons yet alive, of great Integrity, Wisdom and Fame.

I have already told you, what an active Rebel this Multiform Sinner was ; but I forgot to tell you, that he was an eminent Promoter of the Western Remonstrance in the Year 1640. To those Principles, he stuck as close, as to the Devil himself ; insomuch, that when the Government of our Church was Restor'd, he avowedly renounced the Communion of it, and endeavour'd to widen the Schism to the utmost of his Power. He could not so much as indure to look upon an Orthodox Minister, but when he met any of them in the Streets, he would pull his Hat over his Eyes, in a Pharisaical kind of Indignation and Contempt.

While

While he was in Prison, he acknowledged his Hypocrisie, by which he had deluded Men and mock'd GOD; declaring, that in all his Life he had never prayed to GOD in private, nor had any Power to speak when he attempted to do it; although he had such an extraordinary and charming Utterance in his solemn Conventicle-Prayers. He also confessed, that he never bow'd his Knee to GOD at his own, or other Mens Prayers; which exactly agrees with his Sisters Relation, of his leaning at his Prayers on his Magical Staff; and none of his own Party can Remember that at any Devotion, even when he seem'd most Rapturous, they ever saw him Kneel. Nay, furthermore, he confessed, which I cannot mention without horror, that his fluency in Prayer, by which he ravished the People, proceeded from the Assistance of the Devil; who, he said, helped him to the Words and Phrases in which he expressed himself. This hath given several Men several ways of Conjecture how it could be done. Some who knew him better than I ever had the unhappiness to do, are of Opinion, that he was the praying Oracle of the Devil, out of whom he Personally spoke. The Reason which they alledge for their Conjecture is, that sometimes the Sound of his Voice, like the sight of Spirits, had something unnatural in it, as if it had not been form'd by the Organs of Speech.

Others think it Reasonable to believe, That he saw all the Words and Expressions in his Prayer successively written by the Devil in the Air. But upon Enquiry, I find that he, like most of the Extemporians, commonly prayed with his Eyes shut; which if it be true, this Hypothesis will never be able to solve those Diabolical Phænomena in their Afraid which is properly called Despair; a Belief that —

Some again think, That the Words and Expressions of his Prayer, were represented by the Devil upon the Stage of his Fancy, after the same manner, as when a Man Dreams he reads such a Letter or Book. But he never was affected with any Consternations, Tremblings, or Abreptions of Mind, which both in true and false Prophets, were the constant Effects of such strong and violent Impressions, as were requir'd to exhibit such unwonted Representations upon the Imagination; nor after his long Prayers were ended, were his natural Strength or Spirits exhausted, as, if his Devotion had been Visionary, they must have been.

Others therefore, considering him as an Apostate from GOD, and as a Vassal and Apostle of the Devil, think it very agreeable to Divinity to assert, That he was immediately

diately, but yet without much violence, inspir'd by the Devil, and helped by him both in the Conception and Utterance of his Prayers. This they conceive, the Evil Spirit might do, like an *assistant Form*, by impregnating his Fancy with Enthusiastical Conceptions, and thereby rendring his Imagination very turgent, and ready to swell above its Banks; which being done by the immediate Operation of the *Evil Spirit*, the wretched ενεργόμενος could not fail to burst forth *in Flumine Orationis*, or a full Torrent of Prayer; and likewise be affected with such moderate Raptures, as yet left him in a condition to understand what he said. Furthermore, to prevent all possible Objections, they say, That if GOD suffer'd the Devil to counterfeit Prophetical Visions, or the true Spirit of Prophecy under the Law, then they know no Reason, why it should be thought Inconsistent with his Goodness, or disagreeble to his infinite Wisdom, to permit him under the Gospel, to counterfeit Inspiration, or the true Spirit of Prayer. But for my own part, had not the Monster himself ascribed his fluency in Devotion to the Assistance of the Devil, I should have wholly ascribed it to the Vigour of his own Enthusiastical Imagination, without any foreign Force. For not only his fluency in Prayer, but the moderate Raptures, and little extatick Fits, into which he was Transported, are explicable by the natural Power of unassisted Imagination, as I could make it out by many Examples; and where a natural Cause alone is sufficient to account for any Effect, I am always sparing to joyn with it a Supernatural Cause.

All the while he was in Prison, he lay under violent Apprehensions of the heavy Wrath of GOD, which put him into that which is properly called Despair; a Despair which made him hate GOD, and desist from Duty to him; and with which the damped Souls in Hell are reasonably supposed to be constantly affected. In this Sense he was desperate, and therefore would admit neither *Church* nor *Conventicle Ministers* to Pray for him, or Discourse with him about the infinite Mercy of GOD, and the Possibility of the Forgiveness of his Sins. Much less could he endure to be Exhorted to Repent, or be brought to entertain any Thoughts of Repentance; telling all the World, that he had Sinned himself beyond all Possibility of Repentance and Pardon; that he was already Damn'd, that he was sure his Condemnation to Eternal Burnings was already pronounced in Heaven, and that the United Prayers of all the Saints in Heaven and Earth, would be vain and insignificant, if they were offer'd to GOD in his behalf. So that when some

Charitable

Charitable Ministers of the City, by Name the present Bishop of *Galloway*, and Dean of *Edinburgh*, were resolv'd to Pray before him for his Repentance and Pardon, against his Consent, he was with much difficulty with-held from interrupting of them in their Devotions, and the posture he put himself in when they began to Pray, was to lye upon his Bed in a most stupid manner, with his Mouth wide open; and when Prayers were ended, being ask'd if he had heard them and attended to them, he told them, *They were very troublesome, and cruel to him; and that he neither heard their Devotion, nor cared for it, nor could be the better for all the Prayers that Men or Angels could offer up to Heaven upon his Account.*

It was his Interest to believe there was no G O D; and therefore to ease the Torments of his Mind, he attempted now and then to comfort, and flatter up himself into this absurd belief. For he was sometimes observ'd to speak very doubtfully about his Existence; in particular to say, That if it were not for the Terrors which he found Tormenting him within, he should scarce believe there was a G O D.

Being with great Tenderness and Compassion besought by one of the City-Ministers, that he would not so resolvedly destroy himself, by despairing of G O D's Mercy, which upon Repentance had been granted to Murtherers, Adulterers, Sodomists, Bestialists, nay, to those that had deny'd Christ; he reply'd, in Anger, *Trouble me no more with your beseeching of me to Repent, for I know my Sentence of Damnation is already seal'd in Heaven; and I feel my self so hardned within, that if I might obtain Pardon of G O D, and all the glories of Heaven for a single wish that I had not committed the Sins, with the sence whereof I am so tormented, yet I could not prevail with my self to make that single wish. And were your Soul in my Soul's stead, you would find your Exhortations impertinent and troublesome, for I find nothing within me but Blackness and Darkness, Brimstone and Burning to the bottom of Hell.* I have been told by very credible Persons, that the Body of this unclean Beast gave manifest Tokens of its impurity, as soon as it began to be heated by the Flames; and certain it is, that after it was Burnt, a Report was presently sent from hence to the Brethren in the *West*, that the Malefactor, who was Burnt for such execrable Crimes, was not *Major Weir*, but another Person who exactly resembled him, and whom the wicked *Prelates* and *Curates* had Bribed to Personate the Godly *Major* (who was said to be gone with a Contribution to the exiled Brethren in *Holland*) and call himself by his Name, This

I   Report

Report was believ'd in the *Weft* for feveral Months, til time difcover'd that the *Major* was no more.

As for *Jane*, this incarnate Devil's Sifter, fhe was very infenfible of her great Sins, and was fo far from Remorfe o Confcience for them, and Defpairing of the Mercy o GOD, as fhe did, that fhe prefum'd too much upon it placing a great deal of Confidence in her conftant adherence to the *Covenant*, which fhe call'd in her Brother *Mitchel*'s Stile, *The Caufe and Intereft of Chrift*. She confeffed indeed, as he did, that her Sins deferv'd a worfe Death than fhe was condemn'd to Dye; but fhe never fhew'd her felf in the leaft concern'd for what might enfue after Death. When fhe was upon the Ladder, fhe befpoke the People in the following Words, *I fee a great Croud of People come hither to Day to behold a poor old miferable Creatures Death, but I trou there be few among you, who are weeping and mourning for the broken Covenant:* And having fo fpoken, fhe threw her felf in greater hafte off the Ladder than a Perfon fhould have done, who was no better prepar'd for another World.

I could tell you many more remarkable Stories of our *Fanatick Zealots*, that have been put to Death for lying with Beafts, and other unnatural Crimes. One not many Years fince was put to Death at *Sterling* for committing Uncleannefs with five individual, among which there were four Species of irrational Animals; and immediately before his Execution, the unclean Wretch protefted againft the *Prelates*, and boafted of his conftant Zeal for the *Covenant*; and fo without declaring any Deteftations of his Crimes, or defiring the People to Pray for him, went of with all Affurance into the other World. I fhould not have related any of thefe Stories, with Reflection on the Schifmat. cal Party, but that nine parts in ten of the horrid Sins, fuch as *Witchcraft*, *Beaftiality* and *Inceft*, are found among them; which hath occafion'd a Proverbial Sarcafm in our Language againft them, *That the Whigs ga to Heaven a Gate of their own*. This is no Hyperbole, but a plain Hiftorical Truth, which our Judges can teftifie, and which may be confirm'd by the Regifters of our Criminal Courts.

And then as for Adulteries and Fornications, thofe common Failings of thefe Pharifees; there are more of them committed, and more Baftards Born within their Country the Weftern *Holy Land* than in all our Nation befides. This is evident from comparing the Parifh Regifters, and the Regifters of the Prefbyteries, or Rural Deaneries o thofe Shires, with the reft of the Parifh, and Prefbytery Regifters in every Diocefs of the Church. Not very long fince, in a Parifh within the Presbytery of *Pafely*, there were no fewer than 17 *Whigs*, who did publick Penance for Fornications and Adulteries, at one time. The Parifh is very difaffected, fo that on that Lord's Day, wherein this Herd of Goats did ftand in the Seat of publick Repentance; there were but two Regular Perfons, befides the Minifter and Precentor in the Church. I know you are already wondering, that Fanatical Sinners will do Penance in the *Kirk*, which is as ferious and folemn a piece of Worfhip, as any belongs to the Service of G O D.

Therefore to unriddle the *Paradox* unto you, be pleas'd to take Notice, That if any Fornicator, Adulterer, &c. Contumacioufly refufe to fubmit to Church-Cenfure; his Majefty's Advocate is to purfue him before the Supreme Judicature, or Lords of the Seffion ; who, upon Evidence of his Contumacy, iffue out Order for having him declar'd the *King's Rebel*, that is, to be folemnly Denounc'd an *Out-Law*, with the Sound of an Horn. After the Denunciation, Letters of Caption are direct againft him; fo that if he be taken, he muft be put in Prifon ; and although he be not, he forfeits his Perfonal, and the Annual Revenues of his Real Eftate, and becomes altogether α᾽ πρόσωπος, as *Theophilus*, the *Greek* Civilian, calls *Slaves* and *Minors*, and all that are *Civilly Dead*. Hence an *Out-Law* is almoft in the fame Condition with us, as *Deportatus in Infulam*, was among the *Romans*; he is uncapable of all Civil Employment: He hath no *Head* in Law; he can make no Will or Teftament of his own, nor receive any Benefit by any other Man's. So that our Whigs (like yours, who will be Married by the *Common-Prayer*) choofe rather to mock G O D, and offend their tender Confciences fometimes, than forfeit their Liberty and Eftates.

I am very well fatisfy'd in my own Confcience, that I have done nothing againft the ftricteft Rules of Chriftian Charity, in difcovering the impious Principles and Practices of this Sect: I have done it upon the fame Grounds and Motives, that the Ancient Fathers publifh'd the wicked Lives and Opinions of the more primitive *Hereticks* ; particularly of the *Gnofticks*, who were the Archetype of our Whigs : And the Parallel in moft particulars runs fo exact between them, that I cannot abftain from comparing them together.

Firft then, As the *Gnofticks* were fo call'd from Ψευδώνυμος γνώσις, or Knowledge, falfly fo call'd, and boafted that they were the moft Knowing ; altho' they really were the moft Ignorant of the Chriftian Religion, of any Sect in the

World: So our Whigs ftile themfelves the Knowing Chriftians, and look upon us who adhere to the Church, but as ignorant, filly, formal People, that underftand not Gofpel Myfteries, but are fpoil'd after the Tradition of Men, after the Rudiments of the World, and not after *Chrift.*

Secondly, As the *Gnofticks* pretended to underftand the Scriptures better than all other *Chriftians*; and yet did moft abfurdly and blafphemoufly Interpret them, as *Epipha-nius* hath fhew'd in many particulars: So our *Whigs* pretend to this Gift as their own peculiar Talent; and yet Interpret the Word of G O D as abfurdly, to make it comply with their wicked Opinions, as the *Gnofticks* did to make it Countenance theirs. Mr. *Mitchel's* Papers are full Proof of this Charge, befides the Books I mention'd before.

Thirdly, As the *Gnofticks* fpoke ὑπερογκα, or mighty high Things of *Simon Magus,* equalling him with G O D; fo our *Whigs* fpeak big-fwelling Words of *Baal-berith,* or the *Solemn League and Covenant* ; to which they ridiculoufly Apply, whatfoever is faid of the Covenant of Grace, which GOD made with *Abraham,* and of that Political Covenant which he made with the *Jews,* and of the Counterpart of it; which the *Jews,* or any of their Kings made and re-new'd with G O D; Baptizing their Children into it, as into the Covenant of the Gofpel, and making it the Caufe, and Intereft, and Truth of *Chrift.*

Fourthly, As the *Gnofticks* pretended to be *Chriftians,* and yet in many Things comply'd with the wicked *Jews,* and joined with them in raifing Perfecution againft the Church: So our *Whigs* pretend to be the pureft *Proteftants* in the World; and yet in many Things are real *Papifts,* and now joyn moft Cordially with them to over-throw both our and your Church; which the *Papifts* acknowledge to be the ftrongeft Bulwark againft themfelves, that are in the Proteftant World.

Fifthly, As the *Gnofticks* contumelioufly ufed the Apoftles and Presbyters of the Primitive Church, hating them with the Malice of *Cain,* and gain-faying them among the People after the impudent manner of *Corah,* and oppofing them as, *Jannes* and *Jambres* did *Mofes* and *Aaron*; fo our *Whigs* treat our Reverend Clergy with all imaginable Con-tempt and Barbarity; hating our Bifhops with a mortal Hatred, calling their Government an Ufurpation over GOD's Heritage; and rail at his Majefty, and all other Magiftrates that fupport them; Binding and Re-binding themfelves by a Solemn Oath, to Extirpate the Apoftolical

Function

CPSIA information can be obtained
at www.ICGtesting.com
Printed in the USA
LVHW042057280721
693950LV00005B/254